Literacy Moves On

Also available:

The Writing Classroom, edited by Janet Evans, ISBN 1–85346–721–9
The Literate Classroom, edited by Prue Goodwin, ISBN 1–85346–566–6
The Articulate Classroom, edited by Prue Goodwin, ISBN 1–85346–703–0

Other titles in the Informing Teaching series:

Improving Learning in Secondary English, by Geoff Dean,
ISBN 1–84312–146–8
Literacy through Creativity, edited by Prue Goodwin, ISBN 1–84312–087–9
Creativity in the Primary Curriculum, edited by Russell Jones and Dominic Wyse,
ISBN 1–85346–871–1
Drama and English at the Heart of the Curriculum, by Joe Winston,
ISBN 1–84312–059–3
Making Connections in Primary Mathematics, by Sylvia Turner and Judith
McCullouch, ISBN 1–84312–088–7

Literacy Moves On

Using popular culture, new technologies and
critical literacy in the primary classroom

Edited by Janet Evans

 David Fulton Publishers

David Fulton Publishers Ltd
The Chiswick Centre, 414 Chiswick High Road, London W4 5TF

www.fultonpublishers.co.uk

First published in Great Britain in 2004 by David Fulton Publishers

David Fulton Publishers is a division of Granada Learning, part of ITV plc.

10 9 8 7 6 5 4 3 2 1

British Library Cataloguing in Publication Data
A catalogue record for this book is available from the British Library.

ISBN 1 84312 249 9

Cover illustration by 11-year-old Adam King

Typeset by RefineCatch Limited, Bungay, Suffolk
Printed and bound in Great Britain by Ashford Colour Press

Contents

To Les, my husband . . .
he gives unconditional support at all times.
He is a star!

Acknowledgements

Writing is hard and time-consuming and I wish to thank the writers, each one expert in their field, for agreeing to contribute to this edited volume. The time, effort and expertise they have given is truly appreciated.

Many individuals have influenced me in relation to the subject matter of this book but I would especially like to thank Jackie Marsh and Elaine Millard for opening up the field and inspiring me with their wonderfully organised research seminars on popular culture.

When I have needed moral support and a listening ear several people have been there for me. I would particularly like to mention Guy Merchant who has talked things through and given advice on several occasions. Also Anne Thompson, a valued friend and teacher who gives freely of her time and challenges my ideas when appropriate.

I would like to thank my editors Margaret Marriott from David Fulton and Danny Miller from Heinemann. Once again it has been great working with them both. Their advice and encouragement has been welcome – and needed – at all times.

Finally I have two special mentions to make. The first goes to Anne Haas Dyson – the doyenne of research into popular culture. I have really valued her caring involvement and am grateful for her thought-provoking foreword. The second to the children and staff of Gilded Hollins County Primary School, Leigh, Lancashire, who got involved and were willing to talk, write, draw and share ideas when asked. Thanks to all of you.

Janet Evans
September 2004

Foreword

Anne Haas Dyson

In this lively book, Janet Evans and her colleagues offer us, their readers, an imaginative reinterpretation of the longstanding mantra of childhood education: Start where 'the child' is. Their collective efforts are informed by a fresh perspective on the usual places to locate that child. Those usual places are in neatly contained geographic locales and along well-marked literacy paths, as 'the child' accrues an ever-increasing basketload of knowledge and skills. (Pity the child from a poor 'locale' who strays from the path, perhaps diverted by the big bad wolf of contemporary media.)

And yet, as the authors herein know, everyday worlds in geographic locales are populated by people who have migrated from somewhere else, and their circulating texts are pulsating with rhythms, images and words that have crossed borders too in their global media reach (Appadurai 1996). Consider, for example, this vignette based on an ongoing project:

> A British author writes a series of books about a boy wizard, which becomes the basis for movie productions, the most recent of which is, in fact, playing just this weekend in mid-Michigan; a group of American school children, of diverse ethnic cultures and similar economic constraints, are anticipating a cinema excursion to view this film, courtesy of their after-school care program. Six-year-old Tionna is going, and envisions herself riding the bus and sharing her popcorn with Makeda (but not Jeanette, which irritates the latter child). Lyron is not going; instead, his father will rent the first Harry Potter movie (which will be cheaper than giving Lyron money for popcorn and soda pop). Ezekial is not going either, because 'my grandma says Harry Potter is about witchcraft.'

Capitalist ventures like Harry Potter become global, transmedia phenomena. Still, how and what those media mean is found in the actions of people, including children like Tionna and her peers, embedded in particular social, economic, political, even religious circumstances (Massey 1998; Dyson 2003). This is no time for simplistic visions of a homogenous melting-pot world . . . or, indeed, of literacy itself.

But this is what we have in the USA and in other nations around the world. In the States, there is increased emphasis on 'the basics' – the sounds and conventions of written standard English – and schools are accountable for children's steady progress on standardised tests. But in a world of interconnected people and media, children gain experience with increasingly multimodal texts, as written language combines with other symbolic material – images, voices, movement (Kress 2003). Moreover, literacy is not a set of skills but a symbolic resource that mediates participation in varied kinds of practices for representing and communicating meaning (Heath 1983; Street 1993).

It would be a (post-)modernist conceit to link the multimodality of children's writing solely to new technologies. Given time, materials and space, young composers quite readily interweave whatever symbolic tools are at their disposal – drawing, singing, gesturing, talking and, yes, writing (Dyson 1988). But, even now, those modalities are usually interpreted and instructionally channelled quite literally into the 'writing process' (whatever the composer's multimodal intentions). Drawing, for example, is dubbed 'planning for writing', even though it might not have been so intended by a child.

As educators, we are in urgent need of a newly conceived language and literacy curriculum, in which we start where children are, in a media-filled world that is increasingly diverse and interconnected. We may begin by using children's experiences with varied media resources as bridges to a more traditional literacy curriculum. But we cannot stop there. As Evans and her colleagues collectively demonstrate, we need curricula in which children and teachers use their cultural and symbolic resources to deconstruct and design texts of varied modalities, that is, curricula in which they make decisions about the symbolic tools and substance that might suit an ever-widening, evolving network of communicative practices. We also need careful research on the nature of such decisions and how they are situated in diverse childhood histories and channelled by varied official and unofficial contextual conditions. And, to inform all of the above, we need rich visions of classroom possibilities, and that is just what Janet Evans and her colleagues offer in abundance.

Inside the chapters to come, readers will meet, among others: four-year-olds making decisions about the production of animated films; young schoolchildren exploiting the representational possibilities of electronic mail, computer games and adventure genres, both screen-based and print-based; immigrant children studying, playing with and producing a popular media genre and, in the process, making the local cuisine a global matter; and teachers and children analysing kid products like Beanie Babies and Pokemon cards and, thereby, considering their own potential for exploitation and power as consumers. In short, readers will find diverse authors coming together with their symbolic and social resources and experiences; jointly, they provide substantive fuel for our critical, imaginative and enjoyable reconstruction of language and literacy work (and play) for and with our children. Enjoy!

Anne Haas Dyson
Michigan State University
September 2004

References

Appadurai, A. (1996) *Modernity at large.* Minneapolis: University of Minnesota Press.

Dyson, A. Haas (1988) 'Negotiating among multiple worlds: The space/time dimensions of young children's composing', *Research in the Teaching of English,* 22 (4), 355–90.

Dyson, A. Haas (2003) *The brothers and sisters learn to write: Popular literacies in childhood and school cultures.* New York: Teachers College Press.

Heath, S. Brice (1983) *Ways with words: Language, life, and work in communities and classrooms.* Cambridge: Cambridge University Press.

Kress, G. (2003) *Literacy in the new media age.* London: Routledge.

Massey, D. (1998) 'The spatial construction of youth cultures', in T. Skelton & G. Valentine (eds) *Cool places: geographies of youth cultures* (121–9). London: Routledge.

Street, B. (ed.) (1993) *Cross-cultural approaches to literacy.* New York: Cambridge University Press.

Notes on contributors

Eve Bearne

Eve Bearne teaches and researches at the University of Cambridge Faculty of Education. Her current research interests are children's production of multimodal texts and gender, language and literacy. She has edited and written a number of books about language and literacy and about children's literature to include: *Making Progress in Writing* (RoutledgeFalmer 2002); *Art, Narrative and Childhood,* co-edited with Morag Styles (Trentham 2003); and *Classroom Interactions in Literacy,* edited with Henrietta Dombey and Teresa Grainger (Open University Press 2003). She is currently President of the United Kingdom Literacy Association.

Barbara Comber

Barbara Comber is Director of the Centre for Studies in Literacy, Policy and Learning Cultures at the University of South Australia. Her research interests include teachers' work, social justice, critical literacies, poverty and education, and school-based collaborative research. She recently co-edited two books entitled *Negotiating Critical Literacies in Classrooms* (Comber & Simpson 2001) and *Look again: Longitudinal studies of children's literacy learning* (Comber & Barnett 2003). She has been a researcher on a number of longitudinal studies of children's literacy development. Her current research, with Barbara Kamler, includes early- and late-career teacher-researchers investigating together how to turn around the problem of unequal literacy outcomes.

Janet Evans

Janet Evans is Senior Lecturer in Education at Liverpool Hope University and a part-time freelance Literacy and Educational Consultant. She teaches on full-time and part-time postgraduate teacher education courses and provides professional development consultancy to individual teachers and whole schools. Her research interests include critical reader response in the picture story texts genre, process writing and interactive writing through role play in the early years, and the impact of popular culture and critical literacies in the primary classroom. She regularly publishes in academic journals and has edited language and literacy books to include: *What's in the Picture: Responding to Illustrations in Picture Books* (Paul Chapman 1998); *The Writing Classroom: Aspects of Writing and the Primary Child 3–11 Years* (David Fulton 2001); and *Writing in the Elementary Classroom: A Reconsideration* (Heinemann 2001). Janet is on the review panel for several academic journals including the *Journal of Early Childhood Literacy*, Sage Publications, and *Language Arts*, NCTE.

Ros Fisher

Ros Fisher is Senior Lecturer in Education at the University of Exeter where she works with initial teacher training students and master's degree students. Her research interests are centred round the role of the teacher in the teaching of literacy to primary/elementary-aged children. She writes regularly in professional and academic journals. She is the author of *Inside the Literacy Hour* (Routledge 2002); joint editor of *Raising Standards in Literacy* (Falmer 2002); and co-author with Maureen Lewis of a book about Curiosity Kits (NCLL 2003).

Margaret Mackey

Margaret Mackey is an associate professor in the School of Library and Information Studies at the University of Alberta, where she teaches courses on contemporary theories and practices of reading and on multimedia texts for young people. She is the author of *Literacies across Media: Playing the Text* (RoutledgeFalmer 2002); and of *The Case of Peter Rabbit: Contemporary Conditions of Literature for Children* (Garland 1998). She is co-editor of *Children's Literature in Education: An International Quarterly*, with responsibility for North America; and has edited a volume of essays for a centennial series: *Beatrix Potter's Peter Rabbit: A Children's Classic at 100* (Scarecrow 2002). She has written many articles on changing patterns in young people's reading behaviours and on contemporary developments in texts for young people in print and other media.

Jackie Marsh

Jackie Marsh is a Senior Lecturer in the School of Education at the University of Sheffield. She is involved in research relating to the use of popular culture and the media in the early childhood literacy curriculum and is the author of numerous publications in this area. Jackie is one of the founding editors of the *Journal of Early Childhood Literacy*. Publications include *Literacy and Popular Culture*

(Sage 2000) co-authored with Elaine Millard; and the *Handbook of Early Childhood Literacy* (Sage 2003) co-edited with Nigel Hall and Joanne Larson. Jackie is currently President-Elect of the United Kingdom Literacy Association.

Guy Merchant

Guy Merchant is a Principal Lecturer and Co-ordinator of the Language and Literacy Research Group at Sheffield Hallam University. His current research focuses on children and young people's experience of popular digital literacy – particularly the use of synchronous chat and interactive communication through email. He has published a number of research studies and produces a variety of curriculum materials in the area of primary literacy. As a founding editor of the *Journal of Early Childhood Literacy* he has a strong interest in the changing nature of literacy and its impact on early childhood. His recent publications include *Developing Primary Language and Literacy – The Co-ordinator's Handbook* (with Jackie Marsh); *Picture Books for the Literacy Hour*; and *Non-Fiction for the Literacy Hour* (with Huw Thomas).

Elaine Millard

Elaine Millard is a Senior Lecturer in Education at the University of Sheffield and a founder member of its Literacy Research Centre and MA in Literacy and Language in Education. Prior to this, from 1968 to 1988 she worked as an English teacher in a wide variety of 11–18 comprehensive schools in Sheffield and Nottinghamshire. Her research interests span issues in the development of literacy at all levels, from early reading and writing to critical literacy. Her research has focused on gender, race and class differences in the development of home and school literacies, including computer literacies. Her publications include *Differently Literate: Boys, Girls and the Schooling of Literacy* (Falmer Press); and *Literacy and Popular Culture: Using Children's Culture in the Classroom*, co-edited with Jackie Marsh (Paul Chapman Publishers).

Helen Nixon

Helen Nixon is Senior Lecturer in the Centre for Studies in Literacy, Policy and Learning Cultures in the School of Education at the University of South Australia. Her research interests include the pedagogies of global media culture and connections between the new information and communications technologies and changing social constructions of literacy and educational disadvantage. She is particularly interested in how children's out-of-school media popular culture interests might be used within a critical literacy/English curriculum. She is editor with Brenton Doecke and David Homer of *English Teachers at Work*

(AATE/Wakefield Press 2003) and has published widely for English/literacy teachers and researchers.

Dominic Scott

Dominic Scott is currently an assistant professor at Millersville University, Pennsylvania, where he lectures in education. Dominic began his teaching career in Belfast, Northern Ireland, at the beginning of 'the troubles'; an experience that profoundly affected his attitude to education, literacy and liberation. He taught in middle schools and high schools in the United States, and became concerned with the inequalites in educational opportunity for poor and minority children. He has spent much of his career in the US working with children and youth at risk of school failure. This commitment brought him to New Mexico, where he worked with marginalised students in alternative schools. He currently serves on the executive board of a charter school in Lancaster, Pennsylvania, that seeks to provide educational opportunities for students of colour who are at risk of school failure, and is active in Good Schools Pennsylvania, a pressure group that advocates equitable school funding.

Vivian Vasquez

Vivian Vasquez is currently an Assistant Professor at American University in Washington DC. Previous to this she was a pre-schoolteacher and elementary schoolteacher in Canada for 14 years. Recent publications include two books, *Negotiating Critical Literacies with Young Children* and *Getting Beyond I Like the Book: Creating Spaces for Critical Literacy in K–6 Classrooms*. She has also published several book chapters and articles in national and international journals including *Language Arts*, *Phi Delta Kappa*, *Journal of Adolescent and Adult Literacy*, *Reading Teacher* and *Reading Today*. She has held appointive and elective offices in scholarly organisations including the National Council of Teachers of English, the American Educational Research Association, the International Reading Association and the Whole Language Umbrella. Her research interests are in critical literacy, early literacy, inquiry and social justice in school settings, and teacher research. Most recently she is engaged in research on critical literacy across grade levels and across the curriculum in a predominantly ESL setting.

Children's voices
Children talking, drawing and writing about their out-of-school interests

Some children between the ages of three and 11 years were asked what their favourite out-of-school interests were and what they liked to do and play with at home. Their responses, which almost without exception identified popular culture as being of prime importance, fell into five categories: film and video, TV programmes, computer games, toys and other activities (see Figure 3 in the Introduction). Not surprisingly the younger three- and four-year-old children preferred playing with toys more than the older groups of children. Every toy was a film or TV programme tie-in and was linked to many of the associated, commercially available collectables, e.g. figures, badges, comics, dressing-up clothes etc. The older children chose films and videos more than any other category, with TV programmes following a close second. Once again their popular culture interests were evident in each and every one of their choices.

Three- and four-year-old children's choices

Morgan 4 years 4 months

I play with my Barbie toy with my cousin Josh. Barbie has pink clothes and shiny, gold beautiful hair. Red lips like a rose. Colourful with a pink dress, a crown and a coach. The coach takes her around so she doesn't have to walk. There's a horse, a girl horse. I push her along and she pulls the carriage.

Caitlin 4 years 3 months

I play on my computer – Barbie game – press numbers and count 1 2 3 4 5 6 7 . . . 13. You use the handle to carry it [the toy computer].

Gareth 3 years 10 months

With my turtle. He's got a mask and green legs. He kills monsters. He's got a sword to batter the monsters, not the good ones.

Tom 4 years 1 month

Batman, he has a belt and bats. I make my Batman toy fly. He has a remote control and when you press the button it can fly out. He throws bats at the Joker . . . he's funny but he's a baddy and I punch him.

Six- and seven-year-old children's choices

Abigail 7 years 2 months

I put Winnie the Pooh because it's funny.

Abigail 7 years 1 month

Scooby Doo. I watch it on TV. I chose Scooby Doo and the Witch's Ghost. I choose Scooby Doo because it is my favourite programme because there is always someone in the costume.

Oliver 6 years 6 months

X Box game – State of Emergency. Michael is in trouble by the police. He has found a weapon. People are holding TV. Lots of things even sacks. Michael has killed two people.

Toby 7 years 4 months

I have chosen Jurassic Park 3 because it is really scary. And the Spinasaurous killed T Rex.

10- and 11-year-old children's choices

Georgia 11 years 0 months

I have chosen Winnie the Pooh because all the characters are really cute and it's great how they all stick together and go on lots of little adventures. There are lots of collectables which are really fun to collect. I have a pencil case, socks, lots of teddies and even the books and videos. I think that he looks so sweet and adorable.

Thomas 11 years 3 months

The Simpsons are a family of five people, (Homer, Marge, Bart, Lisa and Maggie). The programme is brilliant. It is the funniest cartoon I have ever seen. The jokes are hilarious and I could watch them over and over again. I think Homer is just like my dad.

Adam 11 years 4 months

X10 X10 9 is a game on the internet. It's based on fighting. The game is to get as far as possible, fighting your way through stage after stage of full-on fighting. It's not all just fists, they come at you with nunchucs, bamboo canes and many other objects. I chose to write about this because it's the best game I've come across so far. You can find this game on www.alcarcade.com. Then click on cool games and search the list.

Daniel 10 years 1 month

I watch Harry Potter because I enjoyed the books and took an interest in other items such as games, toys and collectables. I think J.K. Rowling (the creator) has a wonderful imagination.

Introduction
The changing nature of literacy in the twenty-first century

Janet Evans

Children's out-of-school interests

Asking children to talk about what interests them usually evokes a positive response – they are very keen to talk about themselves and their likes and dislikes. However, how often do we do this? And how often do we integrate their interests into the school curriculum making them part of the teaching and learning process?

Eight-year-old David and three-year-old Ellie both chose to talk and draw about their out-of-school interest in computer games. David chose the soccer game he plays on his PlayStation (see Figure 1), while Ellie chose one that links with a popular TV programme, *Nickelodeon Junior* (see Figure 2). Both children seem to be computer-literate or, more specifically, computer game-literate.

Over 90 children between the ages of three and 11 were asked what their out-of-school interests were and what they liked to do and play with at home. Their answers were wide-ranging and fell into categories showing films and videos, TV programmes and computer games to be really popular. Toys were popular with the very young children. However 'other activities' were hardly mentioned by any of the ages (see Figure 3).

Only one child chose book reading and no one chose writing or drawing as an out-of-school interest, only two chose imaginary play or outdoor activities. This lack of interest in certain other interests could have been linked to the way the question was asked, since Margaret Mackey in her book *Literacies Across Media: Playing the Text* (2002) found that children's popular culture interests were not chosen to the exclusion of more traditional literacy activities such as reading and writing. She noted that many children were, at any given time, involved with a variety of different types of interests.

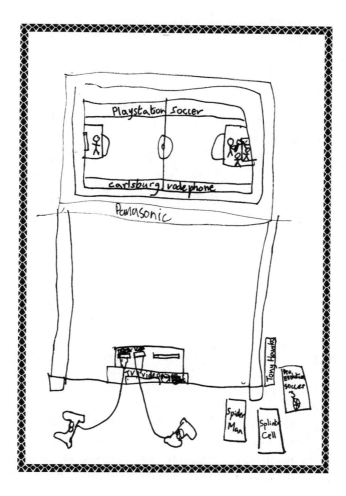

Figure 1

Pro-Evolution Soccer 3 – My favourite PlayStation game

Pro-Evolution Soccer 3 is my favourite PlayStation game. It's really very good. You have to buy the rights for the games. It's like a real match. The crowd blow trumpets that get on your nerves. The players look real and you can do different moves like bicycle kicks and diving headers. Penalties are good because you have to control the goalie and dive for the ball. You can change the formations making substitutions and you end up roaring at the referee because your best player gets sent off – just like Grandad watching.

David (8 years 6 months)

My puppy Blue from Blue's Clues

This is my puppy Blue from Blues Clues. It's [Blue's Clues] on Nick Junior and there's games finding things. If you get five in a row, Swiper, a fox, takes everything out of your backpack. I play on my computer. Some [games] are hard and some not so hard – learning and counting, Buzz Light Year and Little Mermaid games. The Alien one is the hardest, if you need a clue you just click on it.

Ellie (3 years 11 months)

Figure 2

New technologies and the changing nature of literacy

Children of the twenty-first century are fervent users of new technologies, which include computers, DVD, videos, cell phones, email, text messaging etc. These technologies are influencing and changing the activities that children engage with and are in turn influencing and changing literacy. What is evident is that traditional literacy itself is changing and that *new* and *different* literacies, now emerging very rapidly in the first part of the twenty-first century (Lankshear *et al.* 2002), are reflecting these changes 'in technologies, media, the economy and the rapid movement toward global scale in manufacture, finance, communications' (Lankshear & Knobel 2003: 16).

There are assertions that schools are not meeting the demands of today's young people nor are they preparing them for life in an ever-changing world. Despite these complaints most bureaucrats have not reconsidered the curricular demands placed on schools, therefore many education systems in the first decade of the twenty-first century have not changed with the times even though there are well-researched calls for the need for such changes (e.g. State of Queensland 2000). If school-based, traditional literacies have not changed, then the children of this new century certainly have. They are initiating, appropriating and establishing changes to literacy practices in a fast and furious manner. These changes, using the groundbreaking and rapidly developing technological advances of this new century, mean that young children and the youth culture of today are living their lives with and through the aid of digital technology. Lankshear *et al.* (2002) talk of 'technological literacies' to refer to children's use of computers and other

Children's out-of-school and home interests		
3- and 4-year-olds **(28 in class)**	**6- and 7-year-olds** **(29 in class)**	**10- and 11-year-olds** **(34 in class)**
Films and video (2) *Nickelodeon Junior* *SuperMario*	**Films and video (20)** *Scooby Doo (4)* *Lord of the Rings (5)* *Jurassic Park 2: The Lost World (2)* *Winnie the Pooh (2)* *Harry Potter* *Finding Nemo* *Terminator 3* *Gladiator* *The Twits* *The Magic Finger* *ET*	**Films and video (17)** *Winnie the Pooh (6)* *Lord of the Rings (3)* *Titanic (2)* *James Bond* *Finding Nemo* *Jaws* *Dracula* *8 Mile* *The Haunted Mansion*
TV programmes (9) *C-Beebies – Bob the Builder (3)* *C-Beebies – Teletubbies (2)* *C-Beebies – Ballamory* *C-Beebies – Tweenies* *Barnie Bear* *Fimbles*	**TV programmes (8)** *The Simpsons (3)* *Sea Monsters (2)* *Tom and Jerry* *Rachet and Clank* *Scooby Doo*	**TV programmes (6)** *The Simpsons (3)* *Motor Bikes Extreme* *Breed All About It* *The Rugby World Cup preview*
Computer games (3) *Batman game* *Ninja Turtles game* *Barbie computer game*	**Computer games (1)** *State of Emergency – X Box game*	**Computer games (3)** *Roller Coaster Tycoon* *B3TA – games and cartoons website* *X10 X10 9*
Toys (12) *Barbie doll (6)* *Barbie toy bike* *Barbie car* *Bob the Builder figures and outfit* *Batman figures and outfit* *Ninja Turtle figures* *Action Man figures*	**Toys (0)** *None stated*	**Toys (1)** *Barbie collectables*
Other activities (2) *Scooter – playing outside* *Bike – playing outside*	**Other activities (0)** *None stated*	**Other Activities (7)** *Jacqueline Wilson books* *Music (general interest)* *Netball (general interest)* *Compilation – different activities from the above list (4)*

Figure 3

technologies such as videos, video games, compact discs, cell phones, DVDs and satellite communications. Guy Merchant (2003 and in this book), documents how children appropriate these 'technoliteracies' in their communication with peers.

This relationship is symbiotic: children and young people use and make demands on the technology available to them and the technological 'goods' are changed and developed seemingly in response to the demand. The two are as one, each feeding, nurturing and growing off the other and both developing and adapting in ways that result in change. What works is accepted and assimilated into the system, rapidly becoming the norm, while what does not work is either adapted and accommodated or left to atrophy and die. This biological analogy is a useful way of explaining how children and young people of the twenty-first century are central to the way in which Western (capitalist) cultures are continuing to develop. Indeed the child's role is pivotal and many new technological advances revolve around their 'needs', interests and requirements. Kenway and Bullen (2001) document the history of the child as a literate consumer and show how, over a period of time, children have been increasingly targeted as a market in their own right. They note that marketers increasingly recognise the importance of reaching children through new media forms – TV, online computer links, Internet shopping etc. – thereby increasing the need for these forms to be constantly developing in order to reach their target audience. What is clear is that children's interest in new technologies and their impact as consumers in the twenty-first century is certainly here to stay.

What do we mean by texts? The multimodal nature of texts

The definition of what counts as a text is itself changing, as Eve Bearne mentions in the QCA/UKLA booklet *More Than Words: Multimodal Texts in the Classroom* (Bearne *et al.* 2004) and in her chapter in this book. Previously a text was seen as being 'a passage of print or a slice of speech, or an image' (Lankshear *et al.* 2002: 45), that is, texts were seen as things written down – books, magazines and newspapers. They are now perceived as being much more than this. A text is now seen as a unit of communication that may take the form of something written down but also a chunk of discourse, e.g. speech, a conversation, a radio programme, a TV advert, text messaging, a photo in a newspaper etc. Many of these texts are drawn from children's popular culture and have changed the ways in which young readers expect to read, the ways they think and the ways they construct meaning. Bearne (2003a) notes that, 'Children now have many forms of text available to them; these include sound, voices, intonation, stance, gesture and movement as well as print and image.' Bearne (2003b) also notes that, 'any approach to classroom literacy needs not only to recognise the new forms of text which children meet every day but to give multimodal texts a firm place in the curriculum' (p. 98).

Responding to texts from a socially perceptive standpoint: critical literacy

New and increasingly more accepted definitions of what texts are make us realise that literacy does not take place in a vacuum but includes wider social, cultural, historical and political contexts. All texts are ideological. They are all written from a particular standpoint and as such there is no such thing as an impartial, objective text or a neutral position from which a text can be read, written, viewed or spoken. Consider the headlines from two different newspapers: they may be reporting on the same event but the bias is likely to be very different depending on the reporter's personal viewpoint, reason for writing the report or political affiliation etc. Children must be challenged to respond to texts in a critical manner, to use critical literacy as a tool for asking questions such as who makes rules, who controls and holds power, who devises justice and who creates and writes knowledge. Comber (2001) states that when teachers and children are involved in critical literacy the questions they ask will be 'about language and power, about people and lifestyle, about morality and ethics, about who is advantaged by the way things are and who is disadvantaged' (p. 271). Evans' chapter in this book addresses some of these questions. It is important not just to ask questions but to use critical literacy to get things done. Some five-year-old children with whom Vivian Vasquez was working did just this when they designed posters to challenge the accepted norm that only men and not women could be Royal Canadian Mounted Police. Prior to thinking about and discussing this situation they had just accepted it without question, but their critical literacy work led to some very informed five-year-olds (Vasquez 2003; see also her chapter in this book).

Bridging the gap between children's popular culture interests and school requirements

Despite the irreversible links with new/digital technologies, Lankshear and Knobel (2003) draw our attention to the existence of those with 'mindsets forged in physical space and the mechanical age and those forged in cyberspace and the digital age' (p.18). They discuss the need to 'bring the stamp of the "old" to bear upon what should be "new" ' (p.19) and state that children of the twenty-first century have changed and need catering for accordingly. This fusion of old with new, (Millard 2003) is not easy for many educators who feel that daytime, satellite TV, video games and violent, unregulated computer games are having a deleterious effect on the minds of young children. One teacher of young children said:

> It's quite worrying, all of this exposure to unregulated TV, films and computer games. Actually I think it is dangerous, some children are just not getting exposure to good quality books. Even the very youngest children just play with commercial games

and videos all of the time. We are all being led and brainwashed by the big commercial companies.

Lambirth (2003) found that many teachers, some with similar concerns to the one above, were against using popular culture in class. They remembered, with pleasure, the popular culture icons of their own youth. However, their view was that 'They get enough of that at home so they don't need it in school as well'. In a similar vein, Marsh (2003) looked at whether student teachers made use of children's popular culture interests in their curriculum planning. She found that they wanted to but felt they should not as it might be frowned upon. As educators we need to be increasingly aware of the new and different 'worlds' that our children are experiencing – worlds that reflect their social practices and cultures and their day-to-day life. We need to work collaboratively with them in a way that allows us to bridge the gap between the many dynamic, constantly changing worlds in which they live and the older world which is still in existence for many adults – a static world which is seen as an immutable, almost permanent edifice to the twentieth century. To do this we need to find out about, show interest in, and appreciate that children's popular culture interests, their technological expertise, indeed their cultural capital (Bourdieu 1991) are valued in an attempt to make school, currently a legal obligation in most countries of the world, more meaningful for them.

This book has been organised into three parts. The first part consists of four chapters which look at 'new' literacies and children's ways of using them. In the second part three authors share their work focusing on texts with a critical eye; they show how we can create opportunities for critical literacy and identity work. The third and final part looks at three authors who have considered ways in which educators can bridge the gap, making links between children's personal interests and school-based curriculum demands.

Each chapter starts with an overview to 'set the scene' and to help the reader ascertain at a glance what the chapter is about and concludes with an 'implications for practice' section. Each of these sections provides food for thought and offers practical ideas that can be tried in the classroom.

When Rebecca, a 10-year-old child, talked about the things that interested her, she chose a compilation of different interests to include Barbie dolls, Winnie the Pooh video, computer games, Jacqueline Wilson books and buying collectables linked to the above. She justified her choice saying, 'I have chosen all these things because they are all things that I and other children enjoy doing, and when kids play or watch them it makes them feel happy.'

I think we need to be taking notice of Rebecca and making more children happy in relation to using popular culture, new technologies and critical literacy in the classroom.

References

Bearne, E. (2003a) 'Ways of knowing; ways of showing – towards an integrated theory of text', in M. Styles & E. Bearne (eds) *Art, Narrative and Childhood*. Stoke-on-Trent: Trentham Books.

Bearne, E. (2003b) 'Rethinking Literacy: Communication, Representation and Text', *Reading: Literacy and Language*, 37 (3).

Bearne, E., Ellis, S., Graham, L., Hulme, P., Merchant, G. & Mills, C. (2004) *More than Words: Multimodal Texts in the Classroom*. London: QCA/UKLA.

Bourdieu, P. (1991) *Language and Symbolic Power*. Cambridge, MA: Harvard University Press.

Comber, B. (2001) 'Critical Literacies and Local Action: Teacher Knowledge and a "New" Research Agenda', in B. Comber & A. Simpson (eds) (2001) *Negotiating critical literacies in classrooms*. Mahwah, NJ: Lawrence Erlbaum.

Kenway, J. & Bullen, E. (2001) *Consuming Children: Education – Entertainment – Advertising*. Buckingham: Open University Press.

Lambirth, A. (2003) ' "They Get Enough of That at Home": Understanding Aversion to Popular Culture in Schools', *Reading: Literacy and Learning*, 37 (1).

Lankshear, C., Gee, J., Knobel, M. & Searle, C. (2002) *Changing Literacies*. Buckingham: Open University Press.

Lankshear, C. & Knobel, M. (2003) *New Literacies: Changing Knowledge and Classroom Learning*. Buckingham: Open University Press.

Mackey, M. (2002) *Literacies Across Media: Playing the Text*. London: RoutledgeFalmer.

Marsh, J. (2003) 'Taboos, Tightropes and Trivial Pursuits: Pre-service and Newly Qualified Teachers' Beliefs and Practices in Relation to Popular Culture and Literacy.' Paper presented at AERA annual meeting, Chicago, April 2003.

Merchant, G. (2003) 'E-mail me your thoughts: Digital Communication and Narrative Writing', *Reading: Literacy and Language*, 37 (3).

Millard, E. (2003) 'Towards a Literacy of Fusion: New Times, New Teaching and Learning?' *Reading: Literacy and Learning*, 37 (1).

State of Queensland, Department of Education (2000) *Literate Futures: Report of the Literacy Review for Queensland State Schools*, available at: http://www.education.qld.gov.au.

Vasquez, V. (2003) 'Pairing Everyday Texts with Texts Written for Children', in V. Vasquez (2003) *Getting Beyond 'I Like the Book': Creating Space for Critical Literacy in K–6 Classrooms*. Delaware: International Reading Association.

PART 1

'New' literacies and children's ways of using them

'New'/different literacies include screen-based literacies, computer texts and games, video games, text messaging, artefacts and toys etc. They embrace new advances in technology, sometimes called digital literacy or technological (techno) literacy, and include a wider, more embracing definition of 'texts' to include multimodal texts. These communicate in different ways using visual images, drawings, sounds, words. Even the space we inhabit, gestures, body movements are now being considered as texts. This section contains work with children in relation to some of these 'new' literacies.

CHAPTER 1

Multimodal texts
What they are and how children use them

Eve Bearne

Recent developments in digital technology have prompted a reappraisal of just what 'literacy' might mean. 'Reading' now includes more pictures – still and moving – and the routes taken through reading are perhaps more varied than they were. 'Writing' includes the use of images, diagrams and layout; it is now a matter of design as well as composition. The idea of a 'text' is also being redefined; work on multimodal texts reminds us that there are many dimensions to representation and communication. This chapter explores some of these dimensions and considers the classroom demands made by a redefinition of literacy.

Introduction

We live in demanding times. Transformations in communications mean that the landscape of literacy seems altered out of all recognition. This has implications for teaching. Not only do we need to redefine what 'literacy' involves, but also to note new uses of the term 'text'. There is now a vast range of texts available to young readers in different combinations of modes and media so that 'text' has come to include not only words-plus-images but moving images, with their associated soundtracks, too. Digital technology has increased the number and type of screen-based texts: 3D animations, websites, DVDs, PlayStation games, hypertextual narratives, chat sites, email, virtual reality representations. Many of these combine words with moving images, sound, colour, a range of photographic, drawn or digitally created visuals; some are interactive, encouraging the reader to compose, represent and communicate through the several dimensions offered by the technology. Not only are there new types of digital texts, however, but a massive proliferation of book and magazine texts which use image, word, page design and typography, often echoing the dimensions of screen-based technology. The availability and familiarity of these texts mean that not only do children bring wider experience of text to the classroom, but their immersion in a multidimensional world means that they think differently, too (Salomon 1998; Brice Heath 2000). This means that the literacy curriculum and pedagogy need to be reshaped to accommodate to shifts in communication and children's text experience.

In considering the demands and challenges of the literacy curriculum in the twenty-first century, there is a pressing imperative to get to grips with the texts, the contexts in which they are used and the language surrounding them (Lankshear & Knobel 2003; Snyder 2003). Part of this means genuinely widening the scope of thinking to include home and family experience of texts. Taking account of home literacy experience means acknowledging that children's preferences in popular cultural forms of reading and viewing out of the classroom are part of their own landscape. In the classroom, however, the teacher selects the texts and ensures that they will come under some kind of critical scrutiny. It is in the classroom that children's literacy is – and ought to be – critically mediated by teachers and others involved in literacy education. I use 'critically' in more than one sense: it is, of course, critically important that children have access to their rights in literacy, and that teachers provide for their continuing progress in literacy learning. It is equally important that those rights include the right to read critically and it is essential that teachers take on both senses of the critical as they tackle the literacy curriculum. All of this implies a need to develop new ways of talking about texts – and literacy – and the ways in which they are taught in classrooms. Since many of the new forms of text are encountered outside the classroom, and often at home, talking with children about their own experiences of texts must be part of considering what 'literacy' – and specifically critical literacy – might mean in the twenty-first century.

New forms of communication, and the knowledge of texts brought to the classroom by even the very youngest readers, pose new questions for teaching and learning. Many books available in schools now cannot be read by attention to writing alone. Much learning in the curriculum is carried by images, often presented in double-page spreads which are designed to use layout, font size and shape, and colour to complement the information carried by the words. The 'Dorling Kindersley-type' book, for example, or the style of magazine pages, both of which are designed as a deliberate combination of words and images, are familiar both inside and outside the classroom. These shifts in the use of layout and image require that we rethink literacy and how it is taught. A central demand is to understand the differences and relationships between the logic of writing, which is governed by time and sequence, and the logic of image, which is governed by space and simultaneity. A story or a piece of information only makes sense if it is read in the intended order, whereas all the features of a picture are available to the viewer at the same time.

Inevitably, new combinations of words and images raise questions about whether literacy learning is the same when it happens through the spatial nature of drawings, pictures or other images, rather than through the linear organisation of letters into words or the sequences of speech, it involves asking:

- What can image offer that words cannot and what can writing (or speech) do that image cannot? And what about the fact that most of the texts in the new communication landscape are multimodal, combining word, image and often sound? There are implications here for classroom approaches to reading and writing and, indeed, for assessments of what progress in reading or writing multimodal texts might involve.

- How can 'teaching reading' develop to include all the new types of text that are available? Adults and children alike have a fund of reading experience which seems to be unexplored in many current classroom approaches to reading.

- How does new text experience inform our understanding of children's classroom writing and production of multimodal texts? There are issues about how these are given value, responded to and developed.

In this chapter I want to look at some of the issues raised by trying to tackle these questions and the implications for literacy teaching and learning.

Modes, media and affordances

The first issue – about the different ways that image and word carry meaning – relates to modes of representation: the ways a culture makes meaning through speech, writing, image, gesture, music. Over time, cultures develop regularities, patterns and expectations in any mode(s) of representation. Of course, people use more than one mode to represent ideas. Gesture accompanies speech, and pictures are familiar and established ways of communicating ideas. So it can be argued that texts have always contained multimodal elements or possibilities (Andrews 2001; Bearne 2003; Kress 2003) and that these have been used to engage young learners for centuries. When Comenius composed 'Orbis Pictus' in the seventeenth century, he was driven by a conviction that children learn best from the senses and, particularly from the visual (Comenius 1659). The illustrated book (combining the modes of word and image) has long occupied a central place in the education of young readers. Over time, the different technologies available to a community give rise to a range of media for carrying meaning: book, magazine, computer screen, video, film, radio. Current and future combinations of modes and media in their turn make demands on conceptions of literacy.

In terms of communicating meaning, then, there is an issue about what it is possible to do with one mode or another, or with a combination of modes. It is not only a matter of considering what writing affords or allows for ease of communication or, in comparison, what image offers, but also the pedagogic implications of working with children whose text experience is mainly multimodal. Being aware of the different possibilities for meaning offered by multimodal texts means explicitly discussing how texts work to express ideas. This is equally important when considering a whole text or a single page. When reading, for example, what does a printed book afford as compared with watching a text on television? A comparison between a novel and a film can reveal issues of affordance and how the reader/viewer is positioned in relation to the narrative. With a book, the reader can decide to skip descriptive passages, vary the pace of reading and return to earlier pages to check out details or recapture the narrative flow. Although with a video player there is a review and fast forward device, 'skipping' is rather more difficult (and disrupts narrative meaning rather more). Similarly, since descriptive detail is part of the visual image, it is almost impossible to ignore the descriptive elements. The film does not 'afford' the same reading approach as a book does.

The affordances offered by the different modes and media influence the ways texts are used, returned to, reviewed or reread, and how they are organised and constructed. Different types of text have varying organisational structures, or patterns of cohesion, depending on what the text affords to the reader or viewer. Those that are represented through written narrative or report depend on chronological cohesion so that ideas will be linked by time connectives, for example, *then, later, finally*. Texts that are represented visually or diagrammatically depend on spatial cohesion using visual links, for example, arrows or simply the juxtapositions of blocks of print and pictures or diagrams. Texts relayed through the medium of sound, the single voice of a radio newsreader, for example, also depend on chronological logic but in addition are made cohesive by repetitions which would be redundant in written texts. Texts that are relayed through physical movement, sound and gesture – plays, ballet, opera – combine both spatial and sound-repetitive cohesive devices but in this case the spatial is three-dimensional. Affordance, then, is dependent on the material of texts and is related to the ways they are constructed.

Children's text experience is made up of implicit awareness that it is possible to combine different modes and media to get a message across. Since multimodality is part of children's everyday text experience, there is a pressing issue about the relationship between the kinds of reading and writing fostered in schools and this experience. Particularly, how do we acknowledge and respond to children's increasingly frequent choice of using multimodal texts to represent their meaning? The implications of this question come into clear focus when considering five-year-old Liam's rainforest text (Figure 1.1). The rainforest text was his 'writing plan' for a piece of information text. He drew his pictures first then wrote with guidance. The work was cross-curricular, including art and maths as well as drama and literacy, and a classroom display of the rainforest had been established long before the writing began. Leading up to the writing, the class had read simple texts about the Amazonian rainforest and the teacher had discussed how information is presented, specifically looking at how different texts are presented through words and images.[1]

Figure 1.1

Liam has chosen to make a text with images plus labels and additional verbal information to summarise and communicate what he knows. He adopts a humorous, quirky approach, conveying his ideas through very detailed pictorial information in the many images. His experience as a reader is evident from this text. It is equally clear that he has some implicit understanding of the affordances of image and word in the choices he has made to display some ideas spatially and others through writing. He uses text layout as part of his information structure; the outstretched wing of the parrot points to the wealth of different rainforest creatures depicted, acting as an introduction. The pictures themselves stand as short descriptive items and he uses the white space between the images to separate ideas, rather like punctuation. The layout also indicates his view of relevant themes relating to the rainforest, using the overarching tree, the raindrops and the parrot on the left of the page to establish three key features: the canopy, the dampness and the colourful creatures. He structures ideas and material by balancing the factual information carried by the pictures with the atmospheric detail carried by the writing, presented as a block of text on the right-hand side, rather like the text boxes he will have read in designed information books. Perhaps because it is difficult (certainly for a young text-maker) to depict atmosphere by images, he chooses to describe this in one compound sentence: 'It is hot and dark and sweaty and rainy and steamy.' Through these decisions, Liam shows that he implicitly understands the affordances of different modes.

Looked at in terms of issues about learning, Liam's rainforest text raises questions about teaching and assessing children's production of multimodal texts as distinct from teaching and assessing writing alone. What might have been evident about Liam's knowledge of the rainforest if he had been asked only to *write* about what he knew? His impressive detailed knowledge would very likely not have been acknowledged. In most classrooms, writing, not drawing, is still seen as the means by which learning is expressed and assessed. The pictorial element of Liam's text carries much more information than such a young writer might have been able to convey in writing alone. Added to that, Liam not only knows a great deal about the rainforest but also about the ways in which layout aids understanding. Encouraging children to represent their ideas through multimodal work like this helps them to draw on their personal experience of texts in their everyday lives, revealing their strengths rather than emphasising their difficulties. There are serious implications for teaching and learning here.

Orchestrating multimodal reading

Liam represents his knowledge through the design of his page. He also draws on his knowledge of reading in his rainforest text, suggesting that reading, also, can be seen as 'design' (Kress 2003). It is not unusual to consider viewing pictures as a kind of reading, particularly in the early years of schooling, and the book-based multimodal reading material in classrooms assumes that children can read image-plus-word readily, as Liam has done. However, there are some problems associated with this assumption. Reading words has always been considered something that needs to be taught; is it easier to read images and multimodal texts than words alone? If not, how should multimodal reading be taught? Added to this, progress in reading the printed word is often judged by children reading aloud. Since multimodal texts do not follow the linear direction of print and are made up of images as well as words, they cannot easily be read aloud, as whole texts, although they can be 'told' or narrated. This raises an important question about how children read multimodal texts, as distinct from verbally sequenced narrative or information, and about progress in reading when the repertoire increasingly includes multimodal texts. However, these are challenges, not necessarily stumbling blocks. Indeed, it may be that concerns about young readers apparently finding it difficult to seek inference and to comment on authorial style may be addressed through their growing assurance and fluency in reading image, including gesture and action, in multimodal texts.

So what do readers do when they take in information or narratives from multimodal texts? If reading printed text involves 'multilevel processing' (Rumelhart 1976) at letter, word, syntactic and semantic levels, is the processing more complicated, or much the same, when layout, typographical features and image are added? Attempting to unpick these complexities means considering reading pathways as well as the ways that readers process print.

Gunther Kress describes the differences in reading pathways between designed or displayed text and continuous print as the difference between *showing* and *telling* (Kress 2003: 152). In reading a piece of continuous printed text, a story, for example, the reader is *told* about the relationships between events through a sequence of sentences; in reading an image, the reader is *shown* relationships between ideas or the significance of objects through the placing of images in space. The reading path of the continuous print is clear: along the lines from left to right and from top to bottom (in Western print). In a displayed text, where images, blocks of text, typeface and colour are placed across a double-page spread, for example, the reading path is not so clear. The reader has a choice of pathways, although there are some conventions in Western text organisation that can direct the reader's eye (Kress & van Leeuwen 1996). In complex pictorial or multimodal texts, the reading pathway might be radial. Consider reading a double-page Dorling Kindersley-type spread: where does the eye fall first? It may be on the strong central image or on another area of the page, but what is the reading pathway from then on? It is likely that the eye will roam radially around the page, selecting to focus on aspects of the text that seem important at the time. This may be directed by devices such as arrows or strong vectors in the images, leading the eye rather like signposting. Similarly, a picture book-maker might direct the reader's eye through sequences of frames or present a more open route as in collage-type double pages. These texts present robust demands in terms of describing progress in reading. How can we judge when children are getting better at reading such texts?

There is a further complexity involved in reading whole texts that are multimodally presented. The thematic links in continuous printed texts, such as novels or short stories, are presented through repetitions of words, allusions and references. In picture books such links will be made through images, colour, shape and placing on the page as well, perhaps, as through some verbal cohesive devices. Can these be discussed in the same ways as we might talk with children about reading for inference in printed texts? Helping young readers and viewers to read critically beyond the images as well as reading between the lines of verbal text, demands the development of a vocabulary through which to describe and evaluate meanings created by the relationships between image and word or between images themselves.

The variety of reading paths offered by texts and taken by readers/viewers is worth reflection and discussion (Moss 2001; Unsworth 2001). Experienced readers already have a repertoire of reading pathways into visual texts, yet these are rarely made explicit or taught as part of the reading process. Just thinking about the different ways we read maps illustrates the variety of reading pathway choices according to reading purposes:

- If we want to pinpoint a destination on a map, we might read from the outside edges to a point of intersection.

- If we want to find the best route from where we live, we might move from a central point outwards.

- We might simply browse a map, enjoying the idiosyncrasy of place names with no guiding directional force at all.

- We often refer to the maps in endpapers of books as we trace the narrative depicted.

While these examples suggest that there is rather more to 'reading maps' than might at first be considered, it is also clear that adult, or developed, readers have all this range of experience available for explicit discussion with developing readers. In computer texts, also, experienced readers take equally complex pathways as they seek information or communicate with others. Searching the web often means zigzagging back and forth between screens, making sense of the proffered information through a kind of network of ideas. PlayStation games tend to involve sequential and recurrent pathways, while communicating with others through websites combines networking moves with the creation of meaning as part of a (very fast) process of writing and image dumping. Experienced readers (adults and children) are already capable of following varied reading pathways and so have a fund of knowledge which could inform ways of talking with colleagues and the children themselves about routes through multimodal texts.

Writing and multimodality

Children's experience of multimodal texts is part of their cultural and literacy capital (Bourdieu 1977). They think multidimensionally. When they come to represent their meanings, their self-chosen texts often sing and dance their way off the page as Mia shows in her exuberant text after listening to the music of *Peter and the Wolf* (Figure 1.2).

Figure 1.2   Mia's response to *Peter and the Wolf*

The two-dimensional 'static' images capture sound and movement as Mia adds energy to her image by using comic cartoon-like lines to indicate the bird jumping up and down and the cat trying to leap to safety in the tree, but failing and slowly sliding down leaving claw marks in the bark. Similarly, some children capture sound and action in their writing as Cathy shows in the extracts from her *Foxy Loxy* story (Figure 1.3). She expresses sound partly by the use of letter size and shape, partly by capturing the cadences of told story and song.

At the start of the story she depicts shouting by larger letters; midway through she includes lines from the Danny Kaye song 'The Ugly Duckling': 'then they went with a waddle and a qack and a very very worid tear.' As she reaches the end of her story she loses touch with the reader altogether, just writing the sounds she hears in her mind's ear:

> Don't Ask because that anoys me a lot Ok yyyyyyyes sssssssur alrit then then they meet cheeky leeky hahaha Im comeing Im comeing hes waky ant he yes dethently [definitely?] yer yer see what I mean yer yer Shut up you you Ediot yer yer shut up shut up you ok ok ok ok

One of the classroom implications of children's multimodal experience is the need to make explicit how different modes work and how meaning can be translated from one mode to another. Since accurate and coherent writing is still an important aspect of literacy learning, there needs to be some explicit discussion of how to bridge inner visual or aural experience into a written text which

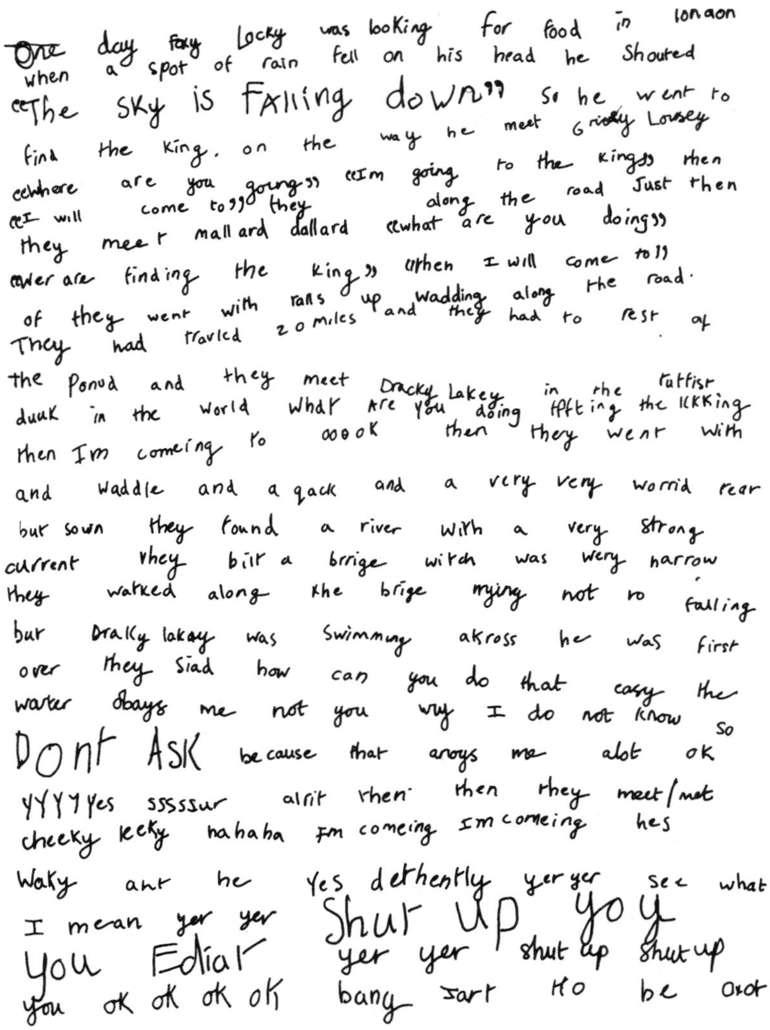

One day Foxy Locky was looking for food in lonaon
when a spot of rain fell on his head he shouted
"The sky is falling down" So he went to
find the king. on the way he meet Griddy Lovsey
"where are you going" "Im going to the kings" then
"I will come to" they along the road Just then
they meer mallard dallard "what are you doing"
"we are finding the king" "then I will come to"
of they went with rans up wadding along the road.
They had travled 20 miles and they had to rest of
the ponod and they meet Dracky Lakey in the tuffisr
duuk in the world what are you doing ffftting the kkking
then Im comeing to cooook then they went with
and waddle and a gack and a very very worrid fear
but sown they found a river with a very strong
current they bilt a brrige witch was wery narrow
they warked along the brige mjing not to falling
but Draky lakay was swimmung akross he was first
over they siad how can you do that easy the
warer dbays me not you wvy I do not know so
Dont ASK because that anoys me alot ok
YYYY yes sssssur alrit then then they meet/met
cheeky keeky hahaha Fm comeing Im comeing hes
Waky ant he yes dethently yer yer see what
I mean yer yer Shut up you
you Ediat yer yer shut up shut up
you ok ok ok ok bang Jart Ho be Orot

Figure 1.3 Cathy's *Foxy Loxy* story

genuinely communicates with the reader. Cathy's story obviously draws on her aural imagination, posing a classroom problem about how to help her move from her inner representation, which depends on the affordances of sound, to the communication of that meaning to others through the mode of writing.

If some children draw on their inner experience of sound, others depend on their visual imaginations as resources for writing and fail to write what they see. Apparently confused or incoherent written texts may be the result of just not making the transformation from inner sight or inner sound to written text. Lee (Year 3) was writing in response to hearing the description of Miss Havisham's house from *Great Expectations* (Figure 1.4).

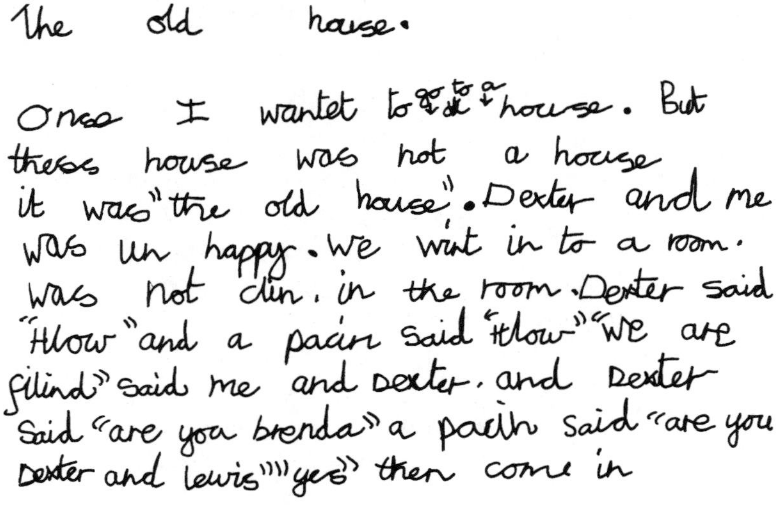

The old house.

Once I wantet to go to a house. But thess house was not a house it was "the old house". Dexter and me was un happy. We wint in to a room. Was not clin. in the room. Dexter said "Hlow" and a pacin said "Hlow" "We are filind" said me and dexter. and Dexter said "are you brenda" a pacin said "are you Dexter and lewis"" "yes" then come in

Figure 1.4   The Old House by Lee aged 7

Clearly it has made an impression on him and he has a strong visual story in his head as he writes:

> Once I wantet to go to a house. But thess house was not a house it was 'the old house'. Dexter and me was un happy. We wint in to a room. Was not clin in the room. Dexter said 'Hlow' and a pacin [person] said 'Hlow' 'We are filind [frightened?] said me and Dexter. And Dexter said 'are you Brenda' a pacin said 'are you Dexter and lewis' 'yes' then come in

This seems very muddled, but if it is separated into sentences, it becomes more coherent and more easily recognised as representing different visual scenes. It reads rather like sub-headings:

> Once I wanted to go to a house.
> But this house was not a house, it was 'the old house'.
> Dexter and me was unhappy.
> We went in to a room.
> [It] was not clean in the room.
> Dexter said, 'Hello' and a person said, 'Hello.'
> 'We are frightened' said me and Dexter.
> And Dexter said, 'Are you Brenda?'
> A person said, 'Are you Dexter and Lewis?'
> 'Yes.'
> Then come in.

Looked at like this, it is quite easy to appreciate the sequence of images which Lee might be drawing on as he sees his narrative unfolding. Cathy's and Lee's writing also indicate one of the implications of multimodality and classroom practice: the need to talk with children about what words and images can do and how to transform inner sound or image into continuous writing.

Conclusion

In rethinking literacy, it is necessary to take into account the dimensions of children's text experience and the ways that new types of text might shape children's thinking. If their experiences are to be genuinely recognised in the classroom, then it is important to discover just what children know about the texts they encounter inside and outside school and the many ways they might represent their ideas. The pace and nature of technological change have had an impact on just what 'reading' and 'writing' have come to mean, so that being visually literate in the twenty-first century will be as important as verbal literacy was in the twentieth century. Literacy teaching now means teaching about multimodality, involving:

- understanding how texts and modes work;
- demonstrating this understanding in the classroom;
- encouraging children to use multimodal representation to shape and communicate their ideas;
- helping children to develop a repertoire of approaches and then to be selective in matching mode with purpose and in making appropriate choices.

Rethinking literacy requires deliberate consideration of how children can be helped to extend and practise their control in different modes by making explicit to themselves – and their teachers – what they know about multidimensional texts and how they work. However, the task is not only to engage in dialogues which will help children recognise the different representational demands made by different texts. It is equally important to develop a community of professional experience – a bank of professional capital – about multimodality. If we are to help learners to move readily between modes, we need a descriptive vocabulary for the several dimensions of texts, including the movement, the sound, the dynamic, implicit in print texts – both visual and verbal. We also need a language of gestural texts and moving image. This raises further questions about how we can develop ways of describing what children know about texts and what progress in multimodality might look like. Perhaps the greatest demand, however, is to imagine a curriculum that helps children to draw on their knowledge of different ways to represent and communicate ideas and that acknowledges and builds teachers' professional expertise – a curriculum for the twenty-first century.

Implications for practice

- Look more closely and identify the different affordances of texts

In tackling issues of the different affordances of texts, children (and adults, perhaps) need to be helped to identify, for example, what a film offers that a book does not or what a picture book allows the reader to do in relation to a video. Take, for example, Raymond Briggs' *The Snowman* or *The Bear*; both are produced in picture book and video form and Briggs was involved in making the video for each, which helps, perhaps, in making comparisons. Careful reading and watching reveal interesting differences: the video of *The Bear* includes a 'prequel' to the picture book narrative. It is worth considering why the prequel was included. It may be related to the possibilities for revisiting a picture book text by flicking the pages backwards and forwards compared with the relative difficulty of revisiting video text. There is, of course, a rewind button but does that afford the same kind of rereading opportunities as the picture book does? There are also video versions of almost every Roald Dahl story: *James and the Giant Peach, Danny, Champion of the World, Matilda, The BFG*. Using these or realistic novels like *Holes* by Louis Sacher allows discussion about the affordances of words and moving images plus sound and colour. Taking an episode of the video and book text allows consideration of how each text creates atmosphere, depicts character or structures the unfolding of the narrative.

- **Think about, observe and describe progress in multimodal text production in the classroom**

Describing progress in multimodal text production is an unfamiliar process for many teachers, yet is a necessary part of rethinking literacy for the twenty-first century. A starting point might be to select a few multimodal texts for children in each year in the school and simply consider if it is possible to identify indicators of development. This would mean thinking about the descriptors that might be used. Can the school's existing assessment framework for ensuring progress in written texts helpfully be applied to multimodal texts? What does not apply at all? What needs to be added? Consideration of these questions might help in developing assessment/record-keeping procedures which genuinely take account of reading and writing multimodal texts.

- **Help children to make choices in relation to the different reading pathways they can take through texts**

Even a brief consideration of possible reading pathways through spatially arranged texts as compared with printed novels, for example, suggests that there is scope for much greater attention to the different pathways that might be taken through a text. This chapter has not even begun to consider hypertextual pathways – for example, the routes taken through website information: are these pathways different from the ways we might access encyclopaedias or textbooks, using indexes and moving between page references as we chase down what we want to find out? It might be worth considering with colleagues the different pathways they, as adults, take through a range of texts, extending the discussion to how the issue of different reading pathways might explicitly be taught. It might be possible, perhaps, to identify some texts that require different reading pathways and to ask young readers to consider how they would tackle the texts. An interesting and more focused investigation might be to select one or two readers and a range of texts and observe the pathways they take as they read. The question then arises: what does this imply for reading instruction?

- ● **What can be done to help children move from one mode to another, e.g. from image and sound to words?**

It is all very well to recognise children's experience in multimodal communication. It is clear that children draw on multimodal models of texts as they shape their own. However, the issue remains about those children who fail to make a transfer between their inner text experience and the demands of writing. Translating from one mode to another does not necessarily come easily. Helping children to make the transition from inner to outer experience might be considered from various directions: from sound to writing; from (moving) image to writing; from writing to image. While information about the detail of children's thinking might be revealed by, for example, reading a passage aloud and asking the class to draw what they hear, the shift from sound to image should not stop there. It is necessary to make explicit how the two modes relate to each other, to consider with the class what is needed for clear communication in each mode, to talk with them about their choices, asking them to explain their decisions about layout, colour, close-up or distance images. This approach could be used with both narrative and non-narrative pieces to see what the differences might be. Translating a piece of video into written form might mean asking the class to retell the action, describe the atmosphere or characters. Discussing the choices they made and the implications of moving between modes and media means an explicit recognition of the different affordances of texts and the accommodations that have to be made when representing ideas in each mode or medium.

Note

[1] My thanks to Liam, Irene Napier and Lynda Graham of Croydon. Liam's text also appears in Bearne *et al.* (2004).

References

Andrews, R. (2001) *Teaching and Learning English*. London: Continuum.

Bearne, E. (2003) 'Ways of knowing; ways of showing – towards an integrated theory of text', in E. Bearne & M. Styles (eds) *Art, Narrative and Childhood*. Stoke-on-Trent: Trentham Books.

Bearne, E., Ellis, S., Graham, L., Hulme, P., Merchant, G. & Mills, C. (2004) *More Than Words: Multimodal Texts in the Classroom*. London: QCA/UKLA.

Bourdieu, P. (1977) *Outline of a Theory of Practice* (trans. Nice, R.). Cambridge: Cambridge University Press.

Brice Heath, S. (2000) 'Seeing Our Way', *Cambridge Journal of Education*, 30 (1), 121–32.

Comenius, J.A. (1659) *Orbis Pictus*, presented by Sadler, J. E. (1968) in facsimile. London: Oxford University Press.

Kress, G. (2003) *Literacy in the New Media Age*. London: Routledge.

Kress, G. & van Leeuwen T. (1996) *The Grammar of Visual Design*. London: Routledge.

Lankshear, C. & Knobel, M. (2003) *New Literacies: Changing Knowledge and Classroom Learning*. Buckingham: Open University Press.

Moss, G. (2001) 'To work or play? Junior age non-fiction as objects of design', *Reading literacy and language*, 35 (3), 106–10.

Rumelhart, D. (1976) 'Toward an interactive model of reading', *Technical Report No. 56*. San Diego Center for Human Information Processing, University of California at San Diego.

Salomon, G. (1998) 'Novel constructivist learning environments and novel technologies: some issues to be concerned with', *Research Dialogue in Learning and Instruction*, 1 (1), 3–12.

Snyder, I. (2003) 'Keywords: a vocabulary of pedadgogy and new media', in E. Bearne, H. Dombey, & T. Grainger (eds) *Classroom Interactions in Literacy*. Maidenhead: Open University Press.

Unsworth, L. (2001) *Teaching Multiliteracies Across the Curriculum: changing contests of text and image in classroom practice*. Buckingham: Open University Press.

Moving stories
Digital editing in the nursery

Jackie Marsh

There are few accounts of media production in nursery or kindergarten classrooms. This lack of attention to key aspects of contemporary ways of communicating has a number of implications for early years educators, the most significant of which is that children's vast experience and knowledge of media is often undervalued and insufficiently developed in schools. In this chapter, work undertaken in one nursery in England is outlined in order to provide a 'telling case' (Mitchell 1994) which can inform teaching and learning in this area. The chapter focuses on the work of four-year-old children as they produce animated films and discusses the relationship between the kinds of skills and knowledge developed in this type of activity and more traditional, print-based literacy practices.

Literacy in a runaway world

In his Reith Lectures of 1967, Dr Edmund Leach, Provost of King's College, Cambridge, talked about a 'runaway world' (Leach 1968), a world that appeared to be changing rapidly and spiralling out of the control of governments and scientists. In 1999, the British sociologist, Anthony Giddens, used the phrase again in his series of Reith Lectures (Giddens 2000) to describe a world in which globalisation was having a major impact on local practices. As knowledge, economies, technologies and populations are transferred across national boundaries at a scale unknown in previous generations, things become a little more uncertain and unpredictable. It is in this global climate of anxiety about what the future might bring that we need to consider the recent changes in literacy practices and explore the implications for educators.

There is now an extensive body of work that has documented how literacy is changing as technology develops the ways in which we communicate (Cope & Kalantzis 2000; Kress 2003; Lankshear & Knobel 2003). However, given this vast body of literature, there still appears to be a lack of clarity with regard to the nature of literacy itself and my aim in this chapter is not to add to the rather confused discourse with regard to the term 'literacy'. Not only is there disagreement about whether literacy is singular or plural (Barton 1994; Hannon 2000; Cope & Kalantzis 2000; Kress 2003), there are also fundamental differences in relation to the specific nature of literacy. Although the concept of 'media literacy' or 'digital literacy' appears to be widely accepted (Buckingham 2003), it is the work of Kress (2003: 23–24) that provides the clearest articulation of the nature of literacy in the new media age. He suggests that literacy relates to lettered representation and that other uses of the term 'literacy' have conflated representational modes and their related resources of production and dissemination (2003: 23). However, while Kress's work in many ways throws clear light on the subject, it has to be accepted that the use of the term 'literacy' to refer to competence in various aspects of new technologies is so widespread that to rein in the meaning would appear to be an impossible task. Certainly, in the development of a theoretical framework for the project described in this chapter, the terms 'digital literacy' (Glister 1997), 'new literacies' (Lankshear & Knobel 2003), 'media literacy' (Buckingham 2003) and 'moving image literacy' (Burn & Leach 2004) were encountered and all appeared to cover some of the same ground, namely the ability to decode and encode using a range of modes of communication including print, still and moving image, sound and gesture, all mediated by new technologies. It is in the move from page to screen that the definitions of literacy become tangled, but for the purposes of this chapter, although it focuses on the screen as the site of composition, the term 'literacy' will be confined to lettered representation (Kress 1997) and other modes of meaning-making referred to as 'communicative practices' (Street 1997).

This chapter explores the digital communicative practices of four-year-old children as they make animated films using a computer. Animated films are created by putting together a series of still images until they give the appearance of movement. They can be created in various ways – through drawings, models and computer graphics, for example – and they form a large part of many children's cultural pleasures, as the popularity of films such as *Toy Story* (Walt Disney Pictures 1995) and *Finding Nemo* (Walt Disney Pictures 2003) suggests. The importance of this kind of activity being undertaken in nurseries, kindergartens and schools is discussed for, as a recent UK publication aimed at introducing early years and primary teachers to work on film and television states, it is 'a simple idea':

> . . . that the moving image – film, television, video and an increasing number of websites and computer games – are important and valuable parts of our culture. It follows that children have a basic right to learn about these media in school.
>
> (BFI 2003: 1)

Despite this kind of learning being perceived by many as a 'basic right', there is still very little work undertaken in the earliest years of school that enables children to learn about some of the most powerful modes of communication in contemporary society. This situation is due to a number of complex factors such as literacy curriculum frameworks which ignore media, the lack of teachers' subject knowledge in this area and a dearth of positive accounts of such work which can be used as illuminating instances of good practice. That is why, in this chapter, the work of teachers in one nursery is documented: such case studies can serve to inform, guide and challenge and thus it is crucial for practitioners and researchers to record instances of work in which traditional notions of literacy are contested (Nixon & Comber 2004). First, however, the extent to which work on the moving image has been incorporated into the literacy curricula of early years classrooms will be explored.

Media education

Work on the analysis and production of moving image (such as films, cartoons, television programmes and advertisements) has traditionally fallen within the remit of media education, or media studies, a subject which is, in some countries, offered to children in the later years of schooling (aged 11–18 years). However, provision for the subject internationally is varied and patchy (Hart 2000; 2001). Hart (2001) discusses the nature of media education in a number of countries including Australia, Canada, Russia and a range of European countries (including England) and suggests that:

> In each case, there are currently different levels of state and regional controls and support, different degrees of professional and material support for teachers and different conceptual frameworks amongst teachers. In all cases, however, the common themes are a lack of curriculum space, absence of support from educational and governmental authorities and a lack of professional training for teachers.
>
> (Hart 2001: 2)

If this is the case with regard to secondary or high school education, the picture in relation to the primary years is even gloomier. There are very little data on the place of media in the primary or elementary curriculum. In addition, it is clear that teacher education for this phase of schooling generally excludes work on media. Hart (2001) has produced the most comprehensive survey to date of the training available for teachers in media education in the UK. The survey focuses primarily on provision for secondary teachers, but Hart does provide evidence of the very limited provision for media in primary Initial Teacher Education (ITE). Hart (2001) surveyed 99 Higher Education Institutions (HEIs) in the UK. Seventy-two online prospectuses were examined for mention of media education and 27 HEIs responded to a survey circulated by Hart:

> In most cases, primary teaching was clearly not included. Where primary teaching was specifically mentioned (five HEIs), two indicated some media education as part of that course (one as a Film Studies module for a BA Education with Qualified Teacher Status, another as one three-hour session amongst 20 sessions in a primary PGCE course).
>
> (Hart 2001: 10)

This presents an alarming indication of the lack of attention paid to media studies by teacher education providers in the UK and it is, therefore, inevitable that the presence of media education in many primary schools is minimal. If this is the case for primary education, then it is fair to assert that media education for pre-school children is, unfortunately, almost unheard of. Indeed, often there is a deficit model presented of young children's competences with the technical aspects of media production. For example, David Gauntlett, a well-respected media theorist who has conducted research projects that have focused on children and media (Gauntlett 1996), states that in one of his projects, children aged seven to 11 were chosen to produce videos on the environment because:

> ... the research had to exclude children so young that we could not expect them to have seen a variety of television material about the environment, or who could not reasonably be expected to do anything meaningful with a video camera.
>
> (Gauntlett 1996: 79)

In a recent review of research which has focused on the analysis and production of the moving image, one important aspect of media education, Burn and Leach (2004) identified only 12 studies in the UK that were relevant to their review and, of these, four involved children of primary-school age. None involved children of pre-school age (three to five years).

This lack of attention in the early years to a range of contemporary communicative practices is of concern, as it is clear that in this post-Fordist society, young people will be leaving school and emerging into the labour force needing a range of skills and knowledge which will equip them sufficiently well for employment in technologically driven, globalised societies (Luke & Luke 2001). In addition, lack of attention to these communicative practices ignores the extensive knowledge of a range of new media, such as computer games and mobile phones, that young children bring with them to nurseries and kindergartens (Marsh 2004). The introduction of media education into early years curricula is, therefore, needed urgently if children are to build successfully on their 'funds of knowledge' (Moll *et al.* 1992) in order to leave school equipped with the understanding required of competent techno-citizens. However, it may be some years before media education as a distinct subject is recognised within nurseries and primary schools. In the meantime, educators should at least ensure that the literacy curriculum includes work on modes of communication other than print. In the work outlined in this chapter, children focused on the moving image.

Burn and Leach (2004) identified four patterns emerging from moving image education in their review of research in the field, which indicated the benefits to be gained from such work: (1) moving image work is located within the socio-cultural interests and experiences of children and young people; (2) work on moving image media leads to gains in literacy (broadly defined); (3) media production can be a collaborative process; and (4) working with moving image media is motivational.

It is, perhaps, the second of these patterns that may be of central importance to readers of this book; moving image education can lead to the development of a range of literacy skills, knowledge and understanding. In a report on a project in which 50 schools introduced digital filming and editing into the curriculum (Reid *et al.* 2002), the authors found that introducing work on moving image media supported the development of a range of transferable skills, including, 'problem-solving, negotiation, thinking, reasoning and risk-taking' (Reid *et al.* 2002: 3). In addition, they determined that the opportunities afforded by animation work were strong because of the way in which children could combine voice, gesture, music, image and language. Therefore, from a review of the limited literature in this area, it can be seen that moving image work in schools can offer a wealth of educational opportunities. In the rest of this chapter, work on digital animation in one nursery classroom is focused upon as a means of closely analysing the benefits to be accrued from moving image education. The choices children made in the activity are explored in order to determine the kinds of communicative practices that are fostered in such work and to understand the affordances of the materials with which they engaged.

The context

The study was undertaken in a nursery in the north of England. The nursery serves very diverse racial and linguistic communities, with a large number of refugee families located in the area. It is an area of economic deprivation and high unemployment and thus constitutes the type of catchment area that has families often labelled 'at risk'. However, the concept of 'at-riskness' has been widely critiqued because of its focus on the communities in question rather than the larger socio-political context which creates poverty in the first place (Carrington & Luke 2003). Although many children took part in the animation work, this chapter focuses on the work of only three children, Leah, Chloe and Sofia, who were all four years of age. Leah was an African-Caribbean girl and Chloe a child with dual heritage (African-Caribbean and English); both spoke English as a first language. Sofia's family were refugees from Somalia and she spoke Arabic as a first language. Although Leah and Chloe had access to computers at home, neither had engaged in animation work before. Sofia did not have access to a computer at home.

An 'animation studio' was set up in one corner of the nursery. This consisted of two laptops, connected to which were webcams. There were a variety of props to hand for the animation: toy figures, artefacts and scenery. In some animation projects, modelling clay has been used to shape figures whose limbs are then moved to portray action. However, for young children, this material can create problems as the clay becomes too soft to shape and figures lose limbs as a result of over-handling. Other animation projects involve the production of drawings or cut-outs, but this is a very complicated and involved process for children of nursery age. Because of this, ready-made plastic figures were chosen for this project, familiar toys to children of this age as they are often used for small-world play. The children filmed the plastic figures using webcams, chosen because their small, pod-like shape meant that the cameras could be placed in stable positions by the children and could be operated using the laptops.[1] The children then used a piece of film-editing software, *imovie2*, to edit the animations. Although *imovie2* has been found to have limitations for more advanced moving image production work, such as that undertaken by media studies students in secondary schools (Reid *et al.* 2002), it was a very effective piece of software in the project discussed in this chapter. As the screenshot in Figure 2.1 demonstrates, the page layout of the screen facilitates ease of use. The large screen in the top left enables children to view their film in progress. The rewind, forward, stop and play buttons are all easily recognised and large enough to facilitate ease of use by children still in the early stages of mouse control. The 'shelf' on the right-hand side of the screen is used to store individual still clips; these are then dragged down onto the timeline at the bottom of the screen and placed in a particular order to create the film. Soundtracks can also be previewed beneath this shelf and then dragged down onto the timeline, a simple process which was easily grasped by these four-year-olds.

The materiality of text production – that is, the resources needed to create a range of texts – is of central importance if educators are to provide materials which support children's early meaning-making (Bomer 2003). There is now an extensive body of literature on the range of resources needed for effective teaching of reading

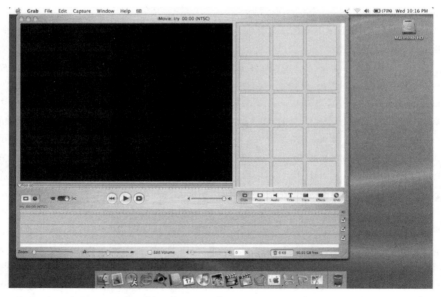

Figure 2.1 *imovie2* screenshot (thanks to Apple Computer Inc. for permission to reproduce this)

and writing (Roskos & Neuman 2001; Makin 2003). Because work on other modes of communication is still in the very early stages in the international arena, there is little guidance on the materials and artefacts that support multimodal text production and analysis. This brief outline of the tools used in this particular activity is, therefore, included only as the smallest of forays into issues relating to the resources needed to undertake moving image work in early years classrooms; it is hoped that this aspect of the early years curriculum will receive more intensive attention in the years ahead.

Making the stories

Leah, Chloe and Sofia played with the equipment over a number of sessions. This exploratory, undirected play was felt to be an initial important first stage by the teachers involved, because it enabled the children to test the limits of the materials and to become confident with the technology. As Labbo and Reinking (2003) suggest, such play has an important role in the development of children as competent users of computer technology. The children used the webcams, connected to laptops, to take photographs of the plastic figures. Once they had been shown how to do this, they were able to operate the equipment independently because of the simplicity of the software (which was supplied with the webcam). An adult had then to import the photographs into *imovie2*, because this was a technically complex task. The children were then shown how to undertake basic operations in *imovie2*. As suggested previously, the basic operations were within the competence levels of these children and, once they had been shown how to use the software, they were able to do these independently. Other tasks were more difficult, for example adding transitions from one shot to another and inserting titles, but the children were able to complete these with adult help.

Once the children had become confident with the hardware and software, they were asked to plan a story that they would animate using *imovie2*. All three girls planned stories on paper. These plans included stories that were quite typical for this age group: they included familiar characters drawn from their experiences of family life and all consisted of simple storylines. The stories all contained narratives with a clear beginning, middle and end, and followed the traditional narrative structure with an opening, complication and resolution (see Figures 2.2, 2.3 and 2.4). These plans demonstrate that the children were all at various stages in competence with regard to the technical aspects of writing, with Chloe and Sofia able to represent writing by making marks which were distinguished from drawing, and Leah able to form letter-like shapes.

When these stories were transformed into animated films, all three girls followed the storylines carefully. In the transformation process, which involved shifting these stories from page to screen, a number of interesting patterns emerged. For example, in Chloe and Leah's animated stories, the girls treated each

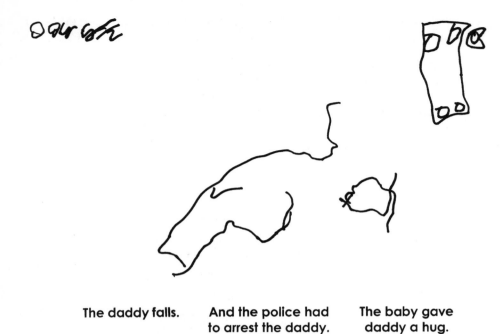

The daddy falls.   **And the police had**   **The baby gave**
                       to arrest the daddy.   **daddy a hug.**

Figure 2.2   Chloe's story

single clip as a scene in itself, rather than understanding that the principle of animation is the presentation of movement frame-by-frame. This was also the case in the animation work that Sefton-Green and Parker undertook with six-year-old and nine-year-old students (Sefton-Green & Parker 2000). In that study, children were more concerned with conveying key points of action in the narrative than portraying movement and this was also the case with two of the four-year-olds

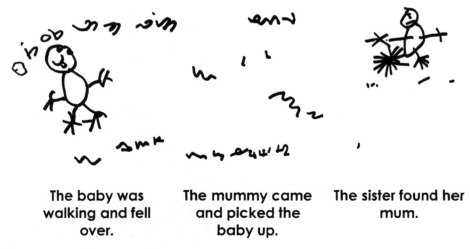

The baby was   **The mummy came**   **The sister found her**
walking and fell   **and picked the**   **mum.**
over.   **baby up.**

Figure 2.3   Leah's story

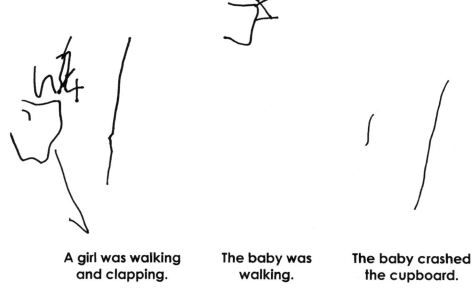

| A girl was walking and clapping. | The baby was walking. | The baby crashed the cupboard. |

Figure 2.4 Sofia's story

in the present study. That, perhaps, reflects the way in which the children were transferring understanding of plot located within print-based narratives to the new mode and they were thus treating the animation activity as if it was the simple transformation of plot from paper to screen. Indeed, there are many similarities across modes and the structuring of stories in both printed and moving image media has been identified as analogous, with narratives in both modes having similar characteristics (Robinson 1997). However, the affordances of these modes are very different and so some fundamental changes occur when moving from one to the other. Kress suggests that the process of shifting across modes can be described as *transduction*:

> This is not the process of transformation, the process which works on a structure and its elements in one mode, but of transduction, a process in which something which has been configured or shaped in one or more modes is reconfigured, reshaped according to the affordances of a quite different mode. It is a change of a different order, a more thoroughgoing change.
>
> (Kress 2003: 47)

The children were asked, once their stories in both media were completed, what they felt were the similarities and differences between their paper and moving image versions. Their answers are detailed in Table 2.1.

I would suggest that this indicates an emergent understanding of the principles of transduction, an understanding which may have been developed by the children's undoubted experiences of encountering narratives in a range of media from an early age (Robinson & Mackey 2003).

Table 2.1 Similarities and differences in the stories across the media, identified by the children

Similarities	Differences
• Characters the same	• Characters move in the animated film
• Same story in both (point related to plot structure)	• The animated film included sounds

Although the evidence from the work of Chloe and Leah suggests that the children found it difficult to understand the durational element of the construction of animated films, in a closer look at the work of one child, Sofia, it is possible to trace an emergent understanding of the nature of animation (see Figure 2.5). The story Sofia planned was detailed in Figure 2.4: *A girl was walking and clapping. The baby was walking. The baby crashed the cupboard.* What is of interest here is the inclusion of the action of clapping. This may have been included because Sofia already knew that she wanted to incorporate the sound of clapping on her soundtrack. She had discovered this sound stored in the *imovie2* sound files when playing with the software and took great delight in playing and replaying it. If she wrote it into her story plan, it could be included in her animated film, and so it was.

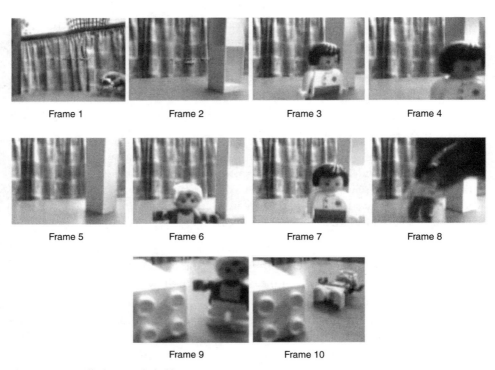

Frame 1   Frame 2   Frame 3   Frame 4

Frame 5   Frame 6   Frame 7   Frame 8

Frame 9   Frame 10

Figure 2.5 Stills from Sofia's film

In Frame 1, Sofia has positioned a key character in her narrative, the baby. Sofia's hand can be seen placing the figure in this clip (and in Frame 8); this occurred because she took the photograph before she had finished positioning the figure. Sofia noted this when playing back her film, exclaiming, in a somewhat disdainful tone, 'My hand's there!' In subsequent animation work, Sofia was careful to take the still image once she was certain her hand or arm could not be seen. This kind of self-correction is, obviously, an important step in learning about a particular medium.

In Frame 2, Sofia introduces another key player in her narrative: the wardrobe. This wardrobe remains in the same place in the next six shots and it is the figures that are placed in relation to this, demonstrating some awareness of the need for continuity. In Frame 3, the girl is introduced. In Frame 4, this figure appears nearer to the camera. This movement from one frame to another is also seen in the transition from Frame 7 to Frame 8. Here, Sofia is portraying movement in time, rather than filming another key part of her plot. In these instances, she was moving beyond the understanding demonstrated by Chloe and Leah, and indeed older children in the study by Sefton-Green and Parker (2000). This understanding is not extended throughout the film, it is emergent; nevertheless it is significant in this context.

The baby is introduced in Frame 6, following a shot (Frame 5) which contains neither character. Sofia may have intended to convey the passing of time from the exit of one character in Frame 4 to the entrance of another in Frame 6, but it is not possible to determine this from the data. In Frames 9 and 10, the baby reappears, indicating a lack of continuity from previous frames. As in her paper-based story, in this animation 'the baby crashed the cupboard' and both baby and wardrobe fall over. Sofia has stuck closely to her narrative structure. Sofia added a soundtrack to this film and the sound of clapping was the first audiotrack to be introduced, as suggested previously. One of the other pre-recorded choices in *imovie2* is the sound of breaking glass and, after listening to all of the choices possible, Sofia clicked on this sound and dragged it onto the timeline. She then recorded her voice retelling the story (*imovie2* enables creators to add two soundtracks simultaneously and, again, she stuck closely to her written narrative. All of this work, apart from the importing of her photographs from the webcam software to *imovie2*, was carried out independently. The animated film was then complete and, although only consisting of ten frames and of 3.7 seconds duration overall, nevertheless was a significant accomplishment for a four-year-old child. The production of such multimodal texts is an important step in understanding the nature and potential of moving image media and is as important to contemporary communicative practices as the print-based activities that are a regular feature of the early years curriculum.

The evidence from the observations undertaken while the children were making the films indicates that the children were enthralled by the process. They all concentrated on the activity for most of the entire duration of sessions (150 minutes), reluctant to join their group sessions at the end of the day. The head of the nursery, Evelyn, was interviewed about the animation work and she suggested that she had been surprised by the children's level of concentration:

> The children were very motivated and keen to take part. This was demonstrated by their concentration – they remained engaged in the activity for quite a sustained period of time – most of the two and a half-hour sessions, in fact. They were also prepared to wait for their turn – giving verbal support to each other while they were watching each other, waiting for their turn to use the equipment. They also remembered from one week to the next. When you came back the following week, not only did they remember what they had done before but stood around waiting for you to get the equipment ready. In fact, I think I had told Sofia in advance that you were coming and so she was watching out for you!

This level of interest and heightened motivation has also been identified in other studies that involved work on moving image (Burn & Leach 2004).

This activity attracted the interest of the children's families. Other studies have also indicated that many parents are supportive of their children's interest in media and new technologies (Dyson 1997, 2003; Marsh 2004). In the work reported in this chapter, the children's families were very responsive to the children's work, as Evelyn noted:

> They enjoyed sharing their successes with each other, other children and staff and with their parents. They got lots of positive feedback from their families which also encouraged them to go on and do more the following week.

Dissonance between the views of educators and parents on the importance of new media in children's lives can lead to incongruence in children's experiences of home and school, which has a number of negative consequences in terms of children's ability to move easily from one domain to another (Makin *et al.* 1999; Marsh 2003). It is important for early years educators to build upon the expertise that children and their families already have in relation to new technologies. Approaches such as the one outlined in this chapter can lead to greater levels of involvement and interest in their children's learning by parents.

In many cases, children's expertise in new technologies outstrips that of parents and other adults. Evelyn commented that the children appeared to be more comfortable with the equipment than some of the adults who were trying to learn how to use the software:

> I thought it was going to be beyond the children's abilities . . . so I was amazed at how well they coped. They picked up the ideas very quickly and could remember the sequence of using the camera and computer. They were not intimidated by any of the equipment, as adults may well be. The second or third week we worked with them, they were able to design their story first and actually followed that up in their animation – I thought they may well have lost the thread so I was impressed when their animation

was similar to their storyboard. If I think back now, Maria (a nursery nurse) and I had more difficulty following the process than the children did!

The confidence the children demonstrated with the hardware may reflect their engagement with technology in the home environment. There is evidence that many young children learn how to operate equipment such as televisions, computers and mobile phones, for example, from a very young age (Gillen, Gamannossi & Cameron 2004; Marsh 2004). This is often in direct contrast with the lack of confidence many adults feel in relation to new technologies and this generational difference has serious implications for pedagogical practice in the new media age (Luke & Luke 2001).

Studies with older children have indicated that digital editing has a number of educational benefits (Reid *et al.* 2002). In this study, the head of the nursery, Evelyn, felt that this activity had developed children's skills, knowledge and understanding in a variety of ways:

> They learnt a lot around literacy, structuring stories and sequencing. It developed their speaking and listening not only in terms of their stories/animations but also in relation to verbally supporting each other – there was a lot of negotiating taking place – whose turn it was to move the figures, operate the equipment, film their story etc. Obviously it developed their ICT skills. Their self-esteem and confidence were given a boost by the responses they received from us, other adults in school and from their families.

There are a number of learning opportunities offered in the development of animated films. In exploring the processes involved in moving narratives from page to screen, Chloe, Leah and Sofia had learnt that stories can be told in a number of media (Mackey 2002); images, sounds and words can be combined to create narratives (Bearne 2003); stories planned on paper can be changed through the transduction process (Kress 2003) into a different medium, this medium having different affordances; and that stories have a beginning, middle and end and can feature one or more characters, in whatever media they are developed. All of these are important lessons in a new media age, as all of the skills, knowledge and understanding identified here are necessary as children begin to navigate the multiple platforms of current technologies (Mackey 2002).

Conclusion

In this chapter, I have outlined a project in which aspects of moving image education were introduced into the curriculum of one nursery. Although it can be seen as a small and isolated example, I would argue that such case studies are able to inform practice in a number of ways. First, an outline such as this can act as a 'telling case', 'which serves to make previously obscure theoretical relationships suddenly apparent' (Mitchell 1994: 239). In this instance, the analysis of the multi-modal production of four-year-old children has illuminated the theoretical concept of *transduction*, albeit in a limited way. Nevertheless, such accounts are needed if we are to fully understand what is involved in the transduction process, and how educators can best scaffold children's experiences in this regard.

Secondly, individual accounts of classroom practice can serve to develop teachers' pedagogical content knowledge (Shulman 1987); it is not enough to know what skills and knowledge children need to develop, one should also be aware of *how* such content is shaped pedagogically. Finally, testimonies of innovative practice extend knowledge about what is possible and raise questions about current curriculum limitations. Only by pushing at such boundaries can educators begin to shape a curriculum that will be relevant for a highly technologised twenty-first century.

Implications for practice

There are a number of implications of this work for early childhood educators. These include the following:

- ### Include media education in the early years curriculum

Media education is vitally important in contemporary society because much of children's daily lives are mediated through new technologies and media texts. Such work can no longer be ignored or marginalised and, therefore, teachers need to develop subject knowledge in this field.

- ### Provide opportunities for children to engage in digital editing

Young children should be encouraged to use digital filming and editing equipment because of the important range of skills, knowledge and understanding it develops, skills which are important for employment and leisure patterns in the new media age.

- ### Compare and contrast versions of the same stories told in different formats, e.g. book, video/DVD, CD-ROM

Teachers need to encourage children to explore and discuss the features of stories in a range of media, identifying the similarities and differences across different modes of representation. In this way, they can develop an understanding of the affordances of different kinds of media.

- ### Encourage children to retell stories using different media

Children need experience in moving narratives from one mode of communication to another. They need to develop skills and understanding in relation to the *transduction* process (i.e. the process of reshaping something which has been configured in one mode into a different mode).

- **Use children's prior expertise in this area as a starting point**

Children's existing knowledge and skills in the use of new media need to be acknowledged and built upon. They arrive at nursery and kindergarten with a sound understanding of and keen interest in these technologies; this should be fostered and extended, not marginalised or ignored.

Although projects such as the one detailed in this chapter are an excellent start to this work, there needs to be greater attention paid to media education in early childhood by governments and policy-makers who are responsible for curriculum development. Children and, in some cases, teachers can continue to bring unbridled enthusiasm for, and expertise in, new technologies to the site of learning, but unless curriculum frameworks reflect these contemporary communicative practices, educational provision will continue to remain out of step with rapid developments in the wider world. There are some isolated examples of such forward-thinking in terms of curricula (e.g. the State of Queensland's *Literate Futures*, 2000), but there needs to be accelerated progress in this area. If this does not occur, then the field of literacy education may never catch up with this 'runaway world' (Leach 1968; Giddens 2000).

Note

[1] The technical advice for this project was provided by Ann Aston, Deputy Head Teacher of Robin Hood Primary School, Birmingham. The work described in this chapter has been undertaken for a number of years in that school with primary-aged children (see http://web.robinhood.bham.sch.uk/ for examples of their pioneering ICT and media work).

References

Barton, D. (1994) *Literacy: An Introduction to the Ecology of Written Language*. Oxford: Blackwell.

Bearne, E. (2003) 'Playing with possibilities: Children's multi-dimensional texts', in E. Bearne, H. Dombey & T. Grainger (eds) *Classroom Interactions in Literacy*. Buckingham: Open University Press.

Bomer, R. (2003) 'Things that make kids smart: A Vygotskian perspective on concrete tool use in primary literacy classrooms', *Journal of Early Childhood Literacy*, 3 (3), 223–47.

British Film Institute (2003) *Look Again: A Teaching Guide to Using Film and Television with Three-to-Eleven-Year-Olds*. London: BFI Education.

Buckingham, D. (2003) *Media Education: Literacy, Learning and Contemporary Culture*. Oxford: Polity Press.

Burn, A. & Leach, J. (2004) 'ICTs and Moving Image Literacy in English', in R. Andrews (ed.) *The Impact of ICT on English 5–16*. London: RoutledgeFalmer.

Carrington, V. & Luke, A. (2003) 'Reading, Homes and Families: From Postmodern to Modern?', in A. van Kleeck, S.A. Stahl & E.B. Bauer (eds) *On Reading to Children: Parents and Teachers*. Mahwah, NJ: Erlbaum.

Cope, B. & Kalantzis, M. (ed.) (2000) *Multiliteracies: Literacy Learning and the Design of Social Futures*. London: Routledge.

Dyson, A.H. (1997) *Writing Superheroes: Contemporary Childhood, Popular Culture, and Classroom Literacy*. New York: Teachers College Press.

Dyson, A.H. (2003) *Brothers and Sisters Learn to Write: Popular Literacies in Childhood and School Cultures*. New York: Teachers College Press.

Gauntlett, D. (1996) *Media, Gender and Identity: An Introduction*. London: Routledge.

Giddens, A. (2000) *Runaway World: How Globalization Is Reshaping Our Lives*. London: Routledge.

Gillen, J., Gamannossi, B.A. & Cameron, C.A. (2004) ' "Pronto, chi parla? (Hello, who is it?"): Telephones as artefacts and communication media in children's discourses', in J. Marsh (ed.) *Popular Culture, New Media and Digital Literacy in Early Childhood*. London: RoutledgeFalmer.

Glister, P. (1997) *Digital Literacy*. New York: John Wiley & Sons.

Hannon, P. (2000) *Reflecting on Literacy in Education*. London: Falmer.

Hart, A. (2000) *Researching Media Teaching in England*. Southampton: Southampton Media Education Group at http://www.soton.ac.uk/~mec.

Hart, A. (2001) *Training Teachers in Media Education in the United Kingdom*. Southampton: Southampton Media Education Group at http://www.soton.ac.uk/~mec.

Kress, G. (1997) *Before Writing: Rethinking the Paths to Literacy*. London: Routledge.

Kress, G. (2003) *Literacy in the New Media Age*. London: Routledge.

Labbo, L. & Reinking, D. (2003) 'Computers and Early Literacy Education', in N. Hall, J. Larson & J. Marsh (eds) *Handbook of Early Childhood Literacy*. London, New Delhi, Thousand Oaks, CA: Sage Publications.

Lankshear, C. & Knobel, M. (2003) *New Literacies: Changing Knowledge and Classroom Learning*. Milton Keynes: Open University Press.

Leach, E. (1968) *A Runaway World: the 1967 Reith Lectures*. Oxford: Oxford University Press.

Luke, A. & Luke, C. (2001) 'Adolescence Lost/Childhood Regained: On Early Intervention and the Emergence of the Techno-Subject', *Journal of Early Childhood Literacy*. 1 (1) 91–120.

Mackey, M. (2002) *Literacies Across Media: Playing the Text*. London: RoutledgeFalmer.

Makin, L. (2003) 'Creating Positive Literacy Learning Environments in Early Childhood', in N. Hall, J. Larson & J. Marsh (eds) *Handbook of Early Childhood Literacy*. London, New Delhi, Thousand Oaks, CA: Sage Publications.

Makin, L., Hayden, J., Holland, A., Arthur, L., Beecher, B., Jones Diaz, C. & McNaught, M. (1999) *Mapping Literacy Practices in Early Childhood Services*. Sydney: NSW Department of Education and Training and NSW Department of Community Services.

Marsh, J. (2003) 'One-way traffic? Connections between literacy practices at home and in the nursery', *British Educational Research Journal*. 29 (3), 369–82.

Marsh, J. (2004) 'The techno-literacy practices of young children', *Journal of Early Childhood Research*, 2 (1), 51–66.

Mitchell, J.C. (1994) 'Case Studies', in R.F. Ellen (ed.) *Ethnographic Research: A Guide to General Conduct*. London: Academic Press.

Moll, L., Amanti, C., Neff, D. & Gonzalez, N. (1992) 'Funds of Knowledge for Teaching: Using a Qualitative Approach to Connect Homes and Classrooms', *Theory into Practice*, 31 (2), 132–41.

Nixon, H. & Comber, B. (2004) 'Behind the scenes: making movies in early years classrooms', in J. Marsh (ed.) *Popular Culture, Media and Digital Literacies in Early Childhood*. London: RoutledgeFalmer.

Reid, M., Burn, A. & Parker, D. (2002) Evaluation Report of the BECTA Digital Video Pilot Project. London: British Film Institute.

Robinson, M. (1997) *Children Reading Print and Television*. London: Falmer Press.

Robinson, M. & Mackey, M. (2003) 'Young children becoming literate in print and televisual media', in N. Hall, J. Larson & J. Marsh (eds) *Handbook of Early Childhood Literacy*. London, New Delhi, Thousand Oaks, CA: Sage Publications.

Roskos, K. & Neuman, S.B. (2001) 'Environment and its Influences for Early Literacy Teaching and Learning', in S. Neuman & D. Dickinson (eds) *Handbook of Early Literacy Research*. New York: Guilford Press.

Sefton-Green, J. & Parker, D. (2000) *Edit-Play: How Children Use Edutainment Software to Tell Stories*. London: British Film Institute.

Shulman, L. (1987) 'Knowledge and teaching: Foundations of the new reform', *Harvard Educational Review*, 57 (1), 1–22.

State of Queensland, Department of Education (2000) *Literate Futures: Report of the Literacy Review for Queensland State Schools*, available at: http://www.education.qld.gov.au.

Street, B. (1997) 'The Implications of the New Literacy Studies for Education', *English in Education*, 31 (3), 45–59.

Walt Disney Pictures (1995) *Toy Story*. Dir: John Lassiter.

Walt Disney Pictures (2003) *Finding Nemo*. Dir: Andrew Stanton.

Children reading and interpreting stories in print, film and computer games

Margaret Mackey

Is a computer game merely a violent time-waster and mind-blower or might it offer new forms of understanding of how stories work? This chapter discusses the interpretive strategies used by a small group of young people playing Douglas Adams' sardonic narrative game, *Starship Titanic*. It then compares their exploration of the confusing game world of a malfunctioning spaceship to ways of approaching other kinds of fiction in print and film. Finally it looks at some implications for teachers.

Introduction

Although we talk about and teach separate interpretive activities – reading, viewing, listening, etc. – people actually live in whole cultures and bring insights from one medium into their approach to another. It is tempting to regard this phenomenon as a particularly contemporary aspect of our multimedia times, but there are many traces of the same concept at work through history. For example, some scholars argue that the development of perspective in painting also affected Renaissance storytelling. As Renaissance viewers/readers learnt to extrapolate and infer the presence of hidden parts of objects in paintings, once perspective was reliably used, so they also learnt to transfer this concept and to extrapolate and infer an ongoing and consistent story world 'between' chapters of a book (Hutson 2003: 3). In the nineteenth century, photography made a serious impact on the print fiction of its day; readers were able to make sense of different kinds of writing in part because photography trained them in new ways of seeing, thinking and responding (Armstrong 2002/1999). Dresang (1999) brings this argument up to date, arguing that 'radical change' means that many books directed at children and young adults take account of new digital elements in our culture: 'Three digital-age concepts underpin and permeate all the radical changes that are taking place in literature for youth: connectivity, interactivity, and access' (p.12). Similarly, Allison Simpson suggests that part of J.K. Rowling's success lies in the fact that she 'is responding to the way kids perceive images in a multimedia world' (quoted in Fray & West 2003).

Many pessimists lament that today's young people decline to read but, instead, 'waste' their lives on 'mindless' and often violent video games. Rather than simply complaining, and writing off a generation of new readers, it is much more constructive, and certainly more interesting, to look carefully at what it is that young people actually know and do as they interact with their games, and to explore ways in which contemporary media affect storytelling assumptions and conventions even for those who do not play games.

In many cases, young people have simply added game-playing and Internet use to the kinds of reading and viewing that have gone on in the past. Much evidence suggests that young people read as much and as well as ever, if not more and better (Wright 2001). And when we look closely at computer games, we see that players must orchestrate many complex reactions in order to navigate the story. Young people today actually read within the framework of a sophisticated context that includes numerous forms of media, multimedia and cross-media engagement.

Learning how to make progress in a computer game is one form of literacy if literacy is broadly defined, and certainly one form of story comprehension. James Paul Gee (2003) has provided an account of his own playing of a number of video games and his exploration of the design and organisation of these games. Gee draws no fewer than 36 educational principles related to learning and literacy, and manifested in the games he explores. It is instructive to compare his account of game-playing with a highly evocative description of fiction reading. George Craig (1997) expresses the complexity of a reader's response in terms that are simultaneously emotional and strategic: 'Shifts of feeling, of energy, of absorption, do not just accompany the act of reading: they are the form of that act for any given instance' (p. 39). Gee (2003) describes similarly contingent, embedded and embodied forms of response in his account of game-playing:

> [V]ideo games honor not just the explicit and verbal knowledge players have about how to play but also the intuitive or tacit knowledge – built into their movements, bodies, and unconscious ways of thinking – they have built up through repeated practice with a family or genre of games.
>
> (p. 110)

In both cases, the authors are describing a temporal submission to the demands of someone else's narrative imagination. In both cases, they outline an activity that requires the orchestration of procedural skills as well as the engagement of some form of emotional empathy – and that duality of decoding strategies and imaginative connection is a feature of any kind of literacy that engages with fiction.

In this chapter, I propose to explore how ways of playing narrative computer games may reflect or alter encounters with other, more established formats. How do skills and strategies acquired from reading or viewing relate to playing? How does playing affect ways of looking at print or film? To explore these questions, I will draw on Rabinowitz's (1987) rules of reading and Douglas and Hargadon's (2001) distinction between immersion and engagement. I will illustrate these points with reference to specific game-playing activities and strategies of young people aged between 10 and 14. (For a more complete description of the game-playing strategies of these young people, see Mackey 2002.)

Gee's (2003) description of his own developing prowess in game-playing is highly instructive for non-gamers, but many of his insights and his capacity to notice and articulate them are those of a late learner – a baby boomer who took up game-playing in adulthood. Young people who have played computer games all their lives are much more likely to have a set of tacit as well as some explicit understandings. Those youngest members of our society who grew up with domestic access to computers may well have learnt to play various digital games over the same time period as they learnt to read, and it would not be surprising to find, in their arsenal of interpretive strategies, a number of media cross-overs that seem completely intuitive to them. At present, adults and children often work from very different backgrounds, making use of quite diverse interpretive toolkits, because they have been exposed to such different kinds of texts. It is important for those adults who wish to understand reading and other forms of narrative interpretation to ponder the implications of what, to them, may effectively be alien frames of understanding. Non-playing adults need to look respectfully at what it is that children actually know how to do with such texts, rather than just assuming the worst.

Conventions of narrative interpretation

Whether or not adults feel intuitively at home in the new textual world, it is important to try to find ways of coming to terms with it. The use of familiar mapping techniques, drawn from print fiction, can be helpful in sorting out new territories. One constructive set of tools comes from Peter Rabinowitz (1987). In his account of narrative interpretation, he draws on examples of nineteenth-century and twentieth-century prose fiction to develop a rubric of interpretive conventions that he calls 'rules of reading'. In a study (Mackey 2002) of five pairs of teenagers playing Douglas Adams' satirical computer game, *Starship Titanic* (Adams 1998), I found that these 'rules' worked well to describe how the players tackled a complex and confusing narrative game. Rabinowitz supplies four sets of rules: rules of notice, of signification, of configuration, and of coherence.

Rules of notice are designed to help readers (or viewers or players) decide what to pay attention to. Even in the most pared-down prose, some details are more significant than others; on the busy screen of a computer game, there is considerable extraneous detail built into the *mise-en-scène*. Conventional pointers (some very obvious) help us to distinguish figure from ground. Rabinowitz offers the example of how we know that the character who speaks first in *Hamlet* (the guard who cries, 'Halt!') is not as significant as the Prince who replies; one major clue is that the Prince's name supplies the title of the play. In prose fiction, first and last sentences in chapters, even in paragraphs, are freighted with extra 'notice' cues. An important sentence can be pointed out by preliminary build-up. Much of how we decide what to pay particular attention to is flagged in ways that we often barely notice, even as we process the significance of the pointer.

Rules of signification are applied to help us decide how to attend to what we have decided to notice. Hamlet is clearly an important character, but should we believe everything he says? What social and psychological assumptions prevail in the fictional world of the play? For example, should we take account of ideas about the divine right of kings as we decide how to interpret his remarks? We make decisions about how to assess the data of the story, often based on information implicit in the text but also introduced from our understanding of the world outside the text.

Rules of configuration help us to put the separate pieces of the story together in a way that offers the potential of making sense. Rabinowitz's short-cut description is that we generally expect that in a story something will happen, but that not just anything can happen in any given story. From the first sentence onwards, stories foreclose some options. Our expectations, often based on convention and genre, lead us to expect certain kinds of outcome. For example, our expectations about a beautiful woman who appears in Chapter 1 may well differ according to whether we judge the story to be a romance or a murder mystery. We expect many things of *Hamlet* from very early in the play, but we do not, for example, anticipate that the hero will change his mind and his life course halfway through the story and start organising a children's playgroup. We notice and signify in accordance with what kind of pattern of events we anticipate, and we put pieces together in order to make sense along the lines of a particular paradigm.

These three groups of rules are applied *during* the process of reading (or viewing or playing) but the *rules of coherence*, by and large, are applied retrospectively, after we have finished the actual encounter with the text. We apply our understanding of the conventions to make the best story we can out of what we have gleaned from our interpretive efforts so far. Thematic connections are worked out, any paucity or excess of information is recast in the best light possible, often also in thematic terms, and so forth. A common example of applying rules of coherence occurs in the post-movie conversation that filmgoers very often engage in, even as they leave the cinema.

All of these approaches, of course, posit a co-operative reader, one who is trying to follow the author's directions to the implied reader. Rabinowitz is certainly aware that readers may be more resistant or critical, but he describes this kind of 'authorial' reading as a model where the rules and conventions are most clearly to be discerned. Even when readers' expectations are not met, he says, the fact of those expectations is part of the interpretive experience.

Applying conventions in a new storytelling format

The computer game of *Starship Titanic*, created by Douglas Adams (1998), who originally made his reputation as a radio dramatist and novelist, draws on all these conventions to create the narrative, but the information that is important to understanding this story appears in many different forms (including print on the screen). Ten young players, aged 13 and 14, who were recorded playing *Starship Titanic* in pairs, made extensive use of these rules, especially the first three sets. (As they were not given time to finish the game, there was no opportunity for them to aim at any kind of global coherence, though there were examples of efforts after local coherence.)

For example, to start the game going, it is necessary to notice and supply significance to visual elements on the screen. The game opens in an elegant home study, with pleasant music playing but no signs of any visible action. Players must first notice that the cursor changes and enlarges into an arrow at the edge of the screen, inviting them to rotate perspective round the study. Next they must observe and ascribe significance to a computer on a desk and the set of CDs lying beside it. To activate the game it is necessary to select the one coloured CD out of the group of silver ones and then to click and drag it to insert it into the computer. This action sets up the initial development of the story as the eponymous starship suddenly crashes through the study ceiling. Subsequently, a robot named Fintible descends to explain the situation. The starship *Titanic* has had its electrics damaged and both the ship's course through space *and* the maintenance of the robots who manage it have been affected. The player is invited to help.

This explanation is conveyed orally by Fintible. Players confirm their intention to assist by typing 'yes' into the dialogue screen. As they enter the starship, communication comes in two forms: the ship's characters speak aloud and their words are also conveyed in print at the bottom of the screen. Players' words are simply typed into the dialogue screen, and their own contribution to the conversation is audible only if players speak their own words aloud as they type.

Exploring the ship, players must attend to visual information and to the explanations of the robots they meet. Deciding on significance is made more difficult because Fintible has already warned players that faulty electronics have made all the ship's robots unreliable. Deciding on what to notice is made more difficult because players have little sense of the kind of story they are involved in. It is an interesting lesson in something that is often invisible in story processing: that conventional or genre expectations about signification and configuration actually affect how and what we actually do notice. We take that process for granted until it fails to work.

It is also striking that players must notice in many different modalities. They must attend to the oral and written words of the robots. They must take note of the shifting visual data as they make decisions about where to move the cursor during their exploration of the ship. They must establish the degree to which they can trust the story itself. For example, when they come across a bomb with a button labelled, 'Press here to disarm bomb', they may learn a major lesson about signification in this fictional world, because pressing the button starts a countdown to explosion.

Jack and Anita, playing *Starship Titanic*, took a long time even to notice that the cursor was inviting them to explore the study. The game stayed completely static, the music repeating and the view of the study remaining unchanged. In a book they might have been able to continue to turn pages, even without understanding very much. However, a book might throw up similar roadblocks (manifested in different ways) if a reader missed the major and vital cues of the first page.

It is interesting to compare the fictional experiences of screen and page. In a game, players must activate developments on the screen. In a book, the words are already fixed on the page. Nevertheless, there are important similarities between the page and the screen, because in both places readers/players must find ways to create that fictional 'lift-off' of the imagination in order for the story to make sense. Mental activation of a set of recorded symbols, which must be assembled over time in ways that make coherent sense according to known conventions, is something that happens in both media.

Immersion and engagement

Another useful way of looking at readers or viewers or players draws on the distinction made by Douglas and Hargadon (2001) between an 'immersed' and an 'engaged' encounter with a text. Immersion, in their account, involves being fully committed to the world inside the text; engagement involves moving inside and outside the text world:

> When immersed in a text, readers' perceptions, reactions, and interactions all take place within the text's frame, which itself usually suggests a single schema and a few definite scripts for highly directed interaction. Conversely, in what we might term the 'engaged affective experience', contradictory schemas or elements that defy conventional schemas tend to disrupt readers' immersion in the text, obliging them to assume an extra-textual perspective on the text, as well as on the schemas that have shaped it and the scripts operating within it.
>
> (p.156)

The distinction between immersion and engagement is a useful one for the discussion of interpretive responses to different media. However, this is not a case where an interpreter is committed to one form of response or another. Many people, in their dealings with a text or set of texts, will alternate between the two categories, and still feel a strong sense of connection to the original story. A single, complex example will illustrate the possibilities. Let us consider a person committed to the world of *The Lord of the Rings*. This person could be completely immersed in reading the books or watching the current movies. Alternatively, or additionally, the person could be immersed in learning some of Tolkien's invented languages, in creating a fan website or in developing a *Dungeons & Dragons*-type game scenario based on the Tolkien spin-offs in this particular game world. On the other hand, there are also many examples of engagement, where the person would move in and out of the narrative schema of *The Lord of the Rings*, exploring the commentaries on the DVD versions perhaps, chatting online about strategies for playing the digital games based on the stories or writing fan fiction that makes use of some of the features and constraints of Tolkien's novels but reworks them into a different story.

Contemporary culture currently fosters an engaged approach to texts somewhat more than a one-off approach of straight immersion. (For a more substantial exploration of how contemporary texts invite play at and across the boundaries of the story world and for some cultural and commercial explanations of this phenomenon, see Mackey 2003.) For today's interpreters of current texts, there are many sources of textual insight, drawn not only from within the text world but also from outside information. Readers, viewers and players are all trained by their culture from a very early age to move between media and apply understandings developed elsewhere to their interpretation of the story itself. Infant readers of *Teletubbies* books apply schemata learnt from their television viewing and from their toys. Adolescent *Spiderman* fans draw on multiple sources of information about the back story, from comic books, from TV interviews, from Internet sites, from supplementary novels and so forth. Engagement as a form of meeting texts is not new, but the contemporary emphasis on engagement as an appropriate approach to many different kinds of story offers us an example of the focus of new media affecting norms of reading. Fifty years ago, young readers were far less likely to resort to numerous sources of outside information as part of their 'normal' reading experience; it is hard not to feel that computer games and DVDs have contributed substantially to this change in approach.

It is instructive to look at the players of *Starship Titanic* as they decide to what extent they should be immersed or engaged in the story. Jack, an experienced player, moved in and out of fictional and strategic modes; he saved his game constantly and readily reverted to an earlier position when he got into trouble, so he had an easy 'out' from local conditions of the fictional universe at any time. Janice and Madeleine, triggering the bomb countdown, enjoyed a histrionic panic over the catastrophe they had set in motion, giving every appearance of being completely immersed in the story, but they concluded their conversation by saying, 'Oh well, if we die we'll start again.' Computer games, perhaps more than any other kind of text, foreground the convention-bound elements of fiction interpretation, and make it possible for players to move easily from reacting inside the story to making strategic decisions in a zone that is outside the story but still inside the game.

In addition, *Starship Titanic* fosters an engaged approach as it certainly cannot be successfully interpreted through the lens of a single or simple schema. Players, at sea in a very confusing but also beguiling world, tap into many forms of understanding as they attempt to make progress through the game. They make use of their understanding of genre conventions (science fiction with a tweak towards the wacky, familiar from many forms of science fiction satire). They also draw on their awareness of tone and register (the whole atmosphere of the starship, sardonically ludicrous and surreal, can be well described as 'Pythonesque' – a mix of silliness, unreliability and casual harshness. Those players who are comfortable in such a foolishly hostile universe fare better). Players also need to be able to work with game-playing strategies (notice and remember as much as you can, even if it makes no sense – you do not know what information you might need later). In the records of my ten players engaging with *Starship Titanic*, they regularly move outside of the story world to discuss how to apply these different understandings in the most productive way; they exit the universe of the story itself but clearly do not leave the zone of the game.

Numerous examples of contemporary print fiction follow this pattern. In today's culture, it is commonplace for readers to have to engage in strategic as well as imaginative approaches to a book. Since at least the time of *Tristram Shandy* (Sterne 1760), novels have challenged their readers to assess how to read them, but such forms of complex reading challenge are far more widespread today.

Reading in a busy world

The multiplication of available media formats means that books exist amid a welter of alternatives aimed at attracting imaginative attention. Fictions abound, and in many cases, the same fiction abounds in many different media. But to consider this undeniable fact as a nightmare scenario of competition in which the silent and undemanding book is guaranteed to wind up in last place is to ignore what is actually happening. In fact, many of the media alternatives often lead back to books, or, perhaps even more powerfully, they lead *from* books, being developed on the premise that the user will already know the book. It is manifestly clear that films, toys, trinkets, Lego kits, Internet sites by the million and a variety of games are not stopping children from reading *Harry Potter*. From the discussions I had with many children around the publication date of *Harry Potter and the Order of the Phoenix* (Rowling 2003), it also seemed very clear to me that the first priority of these child readers was a completely immersed reading, preferably uninterrupted and possibly very rapidly repeated. After this deep immersion in the world of the story, they were open to a more engaged approach, moving in and out of the story world and evidently gaining considerable enjoyment from that movement between the book itself and the commentaries, reviews, chatroom dialogues and maybe even the toys. Among many other elements in contemporary culture, their computer games are teaching them the pleasures of engagement, of a happy alternation between immersion in the story world and temporary movement around and in and out of that world for strategic discussion. (See Mackey 2001 for a fuller discussion of the role of the book in children's contemporary culture.)

Young people and their fictions

Children today live in a world of many fictions. Obviously, adults who work with children in particular local capacities, such as parents or teachers, need to attend to the virtues of reasonable balance and variety in any individual child's life. At a more abstract level, however, I think we benefit from considering a broader picture, one that does not automatically ascribe all the imaginative virtues to the reading of print and equally automatically assume that fierce powers of social depravity are a necessary element in the playing of computer games. Before we can begin to think about the implications for teaching, we need to clarify our understanding of what is actually going on.

The players of *Starship Titanic* draw on complex interpretive skills. Much of what they accomplish as they play this game will leak into other approaches to fiction they may make in a variety of media. Their gaming initiates and refines processes and strategies recognisable to print readers. Playing this game allows them to explore narrative in appealing and challenging ways.

Not all computer games are as narratively sophisticated as *Starship Titanic,* but many games are subtler and more demanding than non-players often assume. As young people move back and forth among the many forms of fiction on offer to them, they are carrying their assumptions about story along with their imaginations. We have much to learn from considering what this process has to offer.

Implications for practice

- Acknowledge student experience and expertise with different narrative forms, even if it is different from your own

The old model of teacher as expert, student as apprentice, is no longer as clear-cut as it once may have been. Whether or not they play digital games themselves, teachers should realise that students in today's classrooms understand the nature of narrative in diverse and complex ways. Creating the understanding of a story from the obscure and confusing elements that make up the experience of *Starship Titanic* is a new kind of narrative challenge. Students who have successfully met this challenge have a broad toolkit of tacit interpretive skills.

- ● Be aware of differences among students and consider the implications for classroom organisation

Of course, not all students in any given classroom will have equal access to such games or equal skill-sets. How can teachers best tap into these implicit understandings and help students to render them articulate, open to critical reflection and thus even more useful?

- ● Take advantage of students' broad experience with more commonmedia forms to help with the exploration of different kinds of narrative understanding

Nearly every Western citizen has some implicit understanding of how to interpret a film. An exercise that invites children to explore ways of telling a given story using words, using moving audio-visuals and using digital forms of interaction would allow everyone to draw on some tacit forms of awareness.

- ● Do not assume expensive technology is necessary

Using classroom equipment to develop a real movie and/or a game from a story would be tremendous fun but probably not realistic in many classroom circumstances. However, a surprising amount of thinking can be generated even just with paper and pencils.

- ● Remember the power of talk

Even simpler is discussion. There are many interesting questions for students to consider. For example, the issue of immersion and engagement is one on which they are bound to hold different views, based on different kinds of experience and also based on the variations of individual psychologies.

- ● Do not waste a fascinating opportunity to look at ways of telling stories

Teachers and teacher librarians have a long (and sometimes ignoble) history of blocking certain forms of text from school consideration (series books, horror stories, comics all come readily to mind). It would be a shame if computer games were similarly excluded, when they offer so much potential for developing a subtler and stronger sense of narrative interpretation.

References

Adams, D. (1998) *Starship Titanic*. CD-ROM. New York: Simon & Schuster Interactive.

Armstrong, N. (2002/1999) *Fiction in the Age of Photography: The Legacy of British Realism*. Cambridge, MA: Harvard University Press.

Craig, G. (1997) 'So Little Do We Know of What Goes On When We Read', in P. Davis (ed.) *Real Voices on Reading*. Basingstoke: Macmillan.

Douglas, J. Y. & Hargadon, A. (2001) 'The Pleasures of Immersion and Engagement: Schemas, Scripts, and the Fifth Business', *Digital Creativity*, 12(3), 153–66.

Dresang, E.T. (1999) *Radical Change: Books for Youth in a Digital Age*. New York: H.W. Wilson.

Fray, A. & West, P. (2003) 'Harry's Magic Is Not By the Book', *Sydney Morning Herald* 30 June. http://www.smh.com.au/articles/2003/06/30/1056824282760.html

Gee, J.P. (2003) *What Video Games Have to Teach Us about Learning and Literacy*. New York: Palgrave Macmillan.

Hutson, L. (2003) 'An Earlier Perspective: What Renaissance Art Can Tell Us about Renaissance Reading', *Times Literary Supplement*, 30 May 3–4.

Mackey, M. (2001) 'The Survival of Engaged Reading in the Internet Age: New Media, Old Media, and the Book', *Children's Literature in Education*, 32(3), 167–89.

Mackey, M. (2002) *Literacies across Media: Playing the Text*. London: RoutledgeFalmer.

Mackey, M. (2003) 'At Play on the Borders of the Diegetic: Story Boundaries and Narrative Interpretation', *Journal of Literacy Research*, 35(1), 591–632.

Rabinowitz, P.J. (1987) *Before Reading: Narrative Conventions and the Politics of Interpretation*. Ithaca: Cornell University Press.

Rowling, J.K. (2003) *Harry Potter and the Order of the Phoenix*. London: Bloomsbury.

Sterne, L. (1760) *The Life and Opinions of Tristram Shandy, Gentleman* (Third edition). London: R. & J. Dodsley.

Wright, R. (2001) *Hip and Trivial: Youth Culture, Book Publishing, and the Greying of Canadian Nationalism*. Toronto: Canadian Scholars' Press.

The Dagger of Doom and the Mighty Handbag
Exploring identity in children's on-screen writing

Guy Merchant

This chapter looks at ways in which children's experience of new technology can help to enrich their construction of narrative. Using evidence from story-making projects, I look at how verbal and visual material is transferred between page and screen when children are given the opportunity to build on their experience of popular culture and new media. This work draws on material from a series of school-based action research projects which have involved the use of interactive email. Archived emails and story fragments are used to illustrate how children borrow and transform the writing practices and voices of others. In their writing, children use popular culture texts and blend them with classroom material to produce hybrid narratives. This raises issues about children's identity as writers and I will argue that on-screen writing offers children new possibilities for performing identity. Children's agency is an integral part of this work, which shows how, despite the institutional constraints of time and space, access to new technology can promote innovation and creativity.

Introduction

There seems to be little doubt that new patterns of social interaction and new literacy practices are emerging alongside the development of new communication technology. The school system varies in its response to this new technology and particularly to the popular communication of email and mobile phone users. In schools and classrooms, policies, practices and pupil cultures influence how on-screen writing is seen and used (Holloway & Valentine 2002). However, dominant conceptions of literacy are still heavily print-based, and professional views about writing on screen are often informed by book-based discourses. As Lankshear, Peters and Knobel (1996) observed:

> Large quantities of electronic hardware and software are currently being employed within pedagogical and curricular practices that merely re-invent the enclosures of book-space within the domain of digital text. In part, the kind of critical practice we envisage calls for appropriate hardware and software. Beyond this, however, it presupposes certain 'awareness' and dispositions on the part of classroom learning communities.
>
> (p.181)

Seven years on, and the dominant paradigm for digital writing in classrooms remains unchanged: it could still be characterised as an enclosure of 'bookspace'. The educational potential of interactive electronic communication has yet to be realised despite a rapid rise in the use and popularity of new technology in the world outside the classroom. Changes in the 'awareness and dispositions' of 'class-room learning communities' are slow to materialise, despite the fact that many children have considerable experience of digital technology. Those who are less fortunate will certainly need access to the new practices involved if they are to participate fully in society (Holloway & Valentine 2003).

Ignoring new communications technology could well increase the polarisation of in-school and out-of-school literacy practices, widening the gap between the school curriculum and the pupils who are taught. Although Dyson's work (1997; 2003) suggests that the curriculum is permeable, by showing the diverse ways in which young children draw on cultural material from their social worlds in the act of writing, it would appear that the importance of classroom culture is critical, particularly with respect to the use of new technology. Indeed, Holloway and Valentine (2002) in their study of ICT illustrate the influence of school policy and teacher practice on the ways in which technology is presented and therefore used in schools and classrooms. I argue that new writing technologies can and should be embedded in the literacy curriculum in ways that recognise children's experi-ences, identities and the literacy practices that surround them (Merchant 2003). Following Hull and Schultz (2001), I suggest that out-of-school identities, social practices and their associated literacies *need* to be incorporated into classroom life if we are to provide an education that is accessible and relevant.

A striking theme that emerges from studies of children working on-screen is the way in which identity is inscribed and enacted through digital writing (Merchant 2003). While this may be common in children's writing, it seems particularly salient at this moment in time when much teaching of literacy is governed by teacher objectives, group and class targets and a model of writing development which is linear and unitary – these being quite particular interpretations of the enclosure of bookspace. By applying Foucault's model of social control we can see how certain literacy practices have become *normalised* – enshrined in the curriculum as official; *seriated* – given a pedagogical progression; and *regulated* through the institution of disciplinary time (Foucault 1977). In other words, the current curriculum highlights specific writing skills, orders how they are to be taught and specifies when this should be done, thus reifying a particular version of bookspace.

An alternative tradition, and one that dates back to the early work of Clay (1975) and Harpin (1976) and resurfaces in the ethnography of Dyson (2003), suggests that this model of literacy development is inadequate, that children's development is essentially non-linear, time-specific and localised. Dyson warns against assuming that 'children are dedicated apprentices hovering exclusively around designated experts' (Dyson 2003: 135) and reminds us of the 'unruliness' of children in their engagements with official literacy in school contexts. Her case studies show how children draw on *different* textual practices, 'recontextualising material from diverse social worlds within official literacy practices' (p. 94). In this model of literacy development, identity and agency are key interrelated elements as the focus shifts from the literacy curriculum to the child as language learner engaged in finding a voice through a variety of social practices.

Wenger (1998) argues that education is about joining a learning community, and that participation in learning communities is concerned with developing or 'negotiating' identity. So Wenger suggests that:

> Building an identity consists in negotiating the meanings of our experiences of membership in social communities. The concept of identity serves as a pivot between the social and the individual, so that we can talk of one in the context of the other.
>
> (Wenger 1998: 145)

This helps us to conceptualise how learners, in this case children, are positioned in multiple social practices and discourses, and how the process of engaging in 'new' discursive practices in the classroom (e.g. writing on screen) may serve to heighten awareness of writing and identity. Written texts and children's identities as writers can be simultaneously constructed in interaction within the specific social context of a writing project.

A useful framework is proposed by Holland and her colleagues (Holland *et al.* 1998). Drawing on their own cross-cultural fieldwork, they develop a theory of identity formation which is characterised by fluidity and improvisation. They:

> ... take identity to be a central means by which selves, and the sets of actions they organize, form and re-form over personal lifetimes and in the histories of collectives.
>
> (Holland *et al.* 1998: 270)

Using a Bakhtinian perspective (Bakhtin 1981), Holland *et al.* define identity formation in terms of 'authoring the self' in dialogic interactions with 'figured worlds'. These figured worlds are essentially contexts for social and discursive practices – so the school, the playground and the home could all constitute figured worlds, and so could some of the microcultures that these contain (the writing curriculum; the computer suite etc.). The individual has both 'positionality' (a power relationship) and agency in a figured world, according to Holland and her colleagues. So as individuals participate in a figured world, they are positioned in it but also have the potential to shape or reconstruct it.

When school curricula are dominated by proscription and enacted through a proliferation of teaching/learning objectives, there is a very real danger that our attention is diverted away from helping young learners to participate in classrooms as learning communities. Opportunities for them to find a voice, and explore identity through writing, may be squeezed into the margins. When children are given permission to write in new ways – and on-screen writing could be considered new, at least in some UK school contexts – it often seems that they engage in the creation of their own counternarratives (Peters & Lankshear 1996) as they explore their identity as writers. It is this notion of writing identity, as it emerges in these counternarratives of digital communication, that is explored here.

Identity and writing

It is possible to identify two aspects of identity and writing. First, there is the idea of a child's 'identity-as-a-writer': this term could be used to describe the process of becoming a member of a community that uses and values writing as a social practice. A developing sense of an identity as a writer involves a recognition of agency and an involvement in social practices and contexts for writing, an understanding of the power of writing and what could be described as a meta-awareness of oneself as a writer.

Secondly we have the idea of 'identity-in-writing' which focuses more on text and text production and specifically the ways in which children's identities and cultural resources are performed and modified in the act of writing. This perspective is not dependent on the meta-awareness described above (although it may inform it) but may be present to some extent in any act of writing or mark-making. Identity-in-writing is used to capture the ways in which written text tells us *about* the writer and who s/he is, wants to be or pretends to be.

This twofold distinction has some similarities with Halliday's thoughts about the *ideational* and *interpersonal* metafunctions of language. In the Hallidayan scheme the ideational relates to reflection: the idea that 'language is about something' and therefore 'encodes cultural experience . . . and individual experience as a member of that culture'. This is complemented by the interpersonal which relates to action: the idea of 'language doing something', expressing 'the role relationships associated with the situation' (Halliday 1978: 112). The emphasis here is on identity, and so the rest of the chapter explores this theme by focusing on 'identity-in-writing'.

Work done with the children

The work reported on here derives from a series of action research projects, which aimed to explore the use of email and on-screen writing in narrative composition. The work was based in three primary schools in South Yorkshire and involved

52 pupils in the seven-to-ten age range in extended classroom writing projects. The projects were based on three popular narrative genres: sword and sorcery adventures, sci-fi stories and myths. Children involved in the writing projects worked collaboratively, composing and writing their own stories on screen.

The projects varied in length, depending on the level of engagement of the young writers, but all involved pupils in a variety of writing activities over a period lasting between three and five weeks. Face-to-face meetings enabled me, and my colleagues, to check progress and maintain interest and momentum in the work. Children were encouraged to email myself and my co-researchers regularly to 'keep in touch', to explain 'how the stories were developing' and to 'ask for advice'. Decisions about when to email were determined by the school context and the enthusiasm of the children. Some of the email correspondence involved children and researchers writing in role.

Children involved in the projects were selected by the participating schools. Their achievements in literacy were broadly in line with national UK standards for writing. ICT provision in the schools was similar in the sense that all classes had access to the Internet. In one school, the children used two computers located in the classroom; in the other two schools, children had regular access to a computer lab. All children had limited prior experience of using email in the school context.

Texts produced by the children were collected and copied. These included drawings, pencil and paper notes used in planning, as well as the electronic files of stories and story fragments. Their emails were archived (a more focused analysis of these can be found in Merchant 2003). A subset of the groups of children involved was selected for interview. These children were interviewed with their writing partner. The audio-taped interviews were conducted in a classroom setting and involved children looking at and commenting on the texts they had produced.

This analysis of the data focuses on verbal and visual features of the texts that convey the complex relationship between identity and writing explored above. A system of classification derived from the data itself is used. This deals with:

- how children introduce themselves either as an actual or virtual presence through their writing (presented under the heading 'Knowing me/Knowing you');
- how the children open and close communication (presented under the heading 'Signing on/Signing off');
- how the children borrow discursive fragments from other texts (presented under the heading 'The Dagger of Doom and the Mighty Handbag').

Knowing me/Knowing you

At a very basic level, all writers are obliged to make choices about how they present themselves to the reader. Whether this is done in a 'direct' way, such as in introducing, or in a coded way when consciously assuming a role or a fictional character, choices of identity or voice are necessarily involved. The boundary between the direct and the coded is, of course, fuzzy. So, for instance, when we introduce ourselves to a prospective employer in a letter of application there is a certain selectivity about what we choose to present. The version of our self in such a letter is not usually a complete fiction, yet at the same time it is unlikely to tell the whole story. Introducing ourselves in what I call a 'coded' way, by creating a virtual persona, also involves selectivity. The choices are usually wider, but there are normally parameters within which our creativity works. It could well be the case that the virtual persona we adopt acts as a skin for another facet of our identity. There is no reason to suppose that children are any exception to this. Young writers make similar choices when writing. Here I begin by examining two examples of children introducing themselves as narrative characters.

First, a traditional approach was adopted by a group of nine-year-old children writing sword and sorcery adventures. They chose pencil and paper to sketch character cards to prepare for on-screen writing. Figure 4.1 shows a virtual character

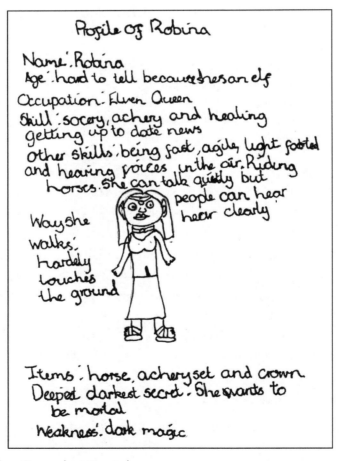

Figure 4.1 Elven Queen character card

created by one of the girls. Modelled on the screen version of Galadriel (as played by Liv Tyler), 'Robina' projects a particular version of femininity which is borrowed and transformed from the Tolkien story and particularly from the screen adaptation.

The layout here is adapted from a trading card of the Pokemon genre, showing the character's defining features, skills and attributes. The central illustration does the work of defining the character – her elven ears, large eyes, full lips and feminine figure. The handle of a dagger shows above the waistband. A long skirt is worn and the outfit is complete with open sandals. The rest of the card details her attributes. The writer alters her name (transforming from Robin to the more feminine-sounding Robina). In all we are presented with an image of how this young writer *wishes to be seen* in her adventure narrative. The card details the character's skills, an intriguing mix of attributes which could be categorised in the following way:

Strong/Hard	Gentle/Soft
archery	healing
being fast	sorcery
agile	light-footed
riding horses	hearing voices in the air
	talks quietly
	hardly touches the ground (when she walks)
	secretly wants to be mortal

```
Chapter 1

3 girls was sent to Jupiter
to kill alien and set the
scientist free the
scientist had herd a nois
coming from her rocket I am
called Rebecca My 2 crew
members are called Helen
and Abi I have got the
green lazer Helen has got
red shiny lazer and Abi had
the blue lazer the
scientist was traped today
because the alien has got
her lets start 5 4 3 2 1
blanst off
```

Figure 4.2   Lazer story fragment

These attributes suggest how the writer perceives herself in relation to Liv Tyler's screen persona (as Galadriel in *The Fellowship of the Ring*). In short, she draws on a multimodal character construct which she then inhabits in her unfolding narrative.

Another strategy popular with young children involves writing themselves directly into the narrative. The characters are displayed 'face-on' in the introduction, with little disguise. In Figure 4.2, two children write themselves into an on-screen narrative using their own names (and introduce a third fictional friend).

This story fragment introduces the authors by name and they, or rather their virtual selves, are transported into the narrative in a manner rather reminiscent of make-believe play. Their preoccupation in this introduction gives emphasis to how they look as they set off on their mission (their choice of laser gun colour) over other considerations. Again this reminds one of the sort of negotiation over props that is often interspersed with socio-dramatic role play.

Two final examples illustrate direct introduction. They are drawn from the email data, and highlight the process of selectivity as well as some specific textual features that are used in interactive online communication. In the first of these (Figure 4.3), two children writing collaboratively introduce themselves to a remote writing adviser assuming the role of a fictional character (for more detail see Merchant 2003). They use their real names, highlight their specific relationship and their group affiliation and then go on to accentuate their playful nature. The modification of the description 'a bit loony' to the accentuated and capitalised 'REALLY loony' suggests multivocality as they supplement their official identity as a part of 'the Myths group'. Further information about the narrative they are

```
To G.,
We are Daisy and Brogan,
We are not sisters just friends.  We are part of the
Myths group, we are a bit loony (no we are REALLY loony).
We have thought of some really exciting ideas : )
We think the beast is like the beast of Beauty & the Beast.
Brogan is happy :-}
Daisy is singing :-0
(me)
We hope you are well because we are.
You're friends :D
Daisy and Brogan xxxxxxxxxxxxxxxxxxxxxxxxxxxxxxxxxxxx
xxxxxxxxxxxxxxxxxxxxxxxxxxxxxxxxxxxxxxxxxxxxxxxxx
xxxxxxxxxxxxxxxxxxxxxxxxxxxxxxxxxxxxxxxxxxxxxxxxx
xxxxxxxxxxxxxxxxxxxxxxxxxxxxxxxxxxxxxxxxxxxxxxxxx
```

Figure 4.3   'We are a bit loony' email

composing makes reference to the Beauty and the Beast story, but this is sandwiched between some highly interpersonal material which perhaps illustrates the emotional tenor of their engagement with the project. The message includes four different emoticons, in turn representing a smile, happiness, singing and laughter as if to convey that they really are loony.

The second email (Figure 4.4) reveals less about the writer's identity. The writer adopts a more direct style following her informal greeting by announcing her group affiliation rather than drawing attention to herself as an individual. Note here how this nine-year-old decides on describing herself as 'one of the *people*' (own emphasis) suggesting a mature identity. The message goes on to suggest that there is plenty to report, but detail is withheld as if to invite further interaction. This is overtly stated with 'Plz mail me back.'

> Hi! Im one of the people from the myths group! My names
> Kavita and we've found alot of strange things! Plz mail me back.
> ~*Kavita*~

Figure 4.4   'One of the people' email

Both of these emails show how interaction through digital text can provide opportunities for children to present or invent themselves in different ways – a theme I return to later on.

Signing on/Signing off

Another very obvious way in which we signal our identity is through our greetings, closing remarks and signatures. As we have seen, 'Hi' is the dominant form of greeting in online correspondence and is usually adopted by children (except when they are less familiar with the medium), although the project archives also include uses of 'To . . .', as in Figure 4.3, and sometimes 'Dear . . .' as in conventional letter writing. However, even 'Hi' can be modified through punctuation and capitalisation to consciously communicate tone. Closing moves tend to show more variation – interestingly, the two emails shown above both invite response – but in rather different ways. In Figure 4.3, the writers obliquely say, 'we hope you are well because we are', prefacing the closing signature with 'You're friends'. The writer in Figure 4.4 uses a more direct approach: 'Plz mail me back.' This again highlights interactivity and the interpersonal function of the messages.

The signature is a fundamental expression of who we are. It is an important marker of our identity and certainly in adult life crosses official and unofficial domains. Creating a signature on-screen, where the distinctive features of handwriting are not usually represented, introduces new challenges for writers. There is plenty of literature on 'handles' (see for example Crystal 2001) and aliases in online communities. Elaborate modifications of email signatures are documented by de Pourbaix (2000) in her study of newsgroups as she shows their link with individual and community identity. An example from the project data shows one child gradually revealing her on-screen identity as she builds a relationship with a remote writing adviser. Figure 4.5 shows a sequence of emails in chronological order.

Email 1

To L,
    The strange things going on are that a couple of days ago I went to play in my garden, and all my flowers weren't there (as its winter) but strangely there was a red rose standing in the bare grass [...] I feel like its trying to tell me something
    From Kavita

Email 2

Hi L its Kavita here, We've marked down where most of the strange things are happening! The strange thing is that most of them are very near the park. In my opinion they might be coming together again. Really spoooooky!!!
    I will be getting pictures if anymore roses come!
    :D :P talk to you later
    ~*Kavita*~

Email 3

Hi! U may not know me well but I'm Kavita and i'm good friends with daisy and Brogan and i think we'll become really g:):)d friends! May not be as looney as them but i am CRAZY!!!!!!! Plz email me back!
    Luv
    xxxxxxx~*Kavita*~xxxxxxx

Figure 4.5   x~*Signatures*~x

The third email shows a visually distinctive signature, with the name symmetrically framed by kisses, swung dashes and asterisks. But this signature is not used in her early on-screen writing; only as the project developed did the characteristic ~*Kavita*~ become a regular and distinctive feature. Here is what she says about it:

> K: I do that all the time on my name when I do my name on the computer and stuff [. . .]
> I put my name like that cos it looks really neat and it looks boring just as a name, and it looks nice . . . looking nice like that [. . .] I haven't on the first one I did [referring to the email] cos I thought it'd look a bit weird [. . .] Then I got used to it looking chatty [. . .]

Kavita is clearly concerned with the visual impact of her messages and the decision to use her on-screen signature seems to represent a development in her relationship with her audience and a willingness to 'show' an aspect of her identity previously restricted to her out-of-school practices which included emailing friends and contributing to discussion boards.

The Dagger of Doom and the Mighty Handbag

Children's capacity to import and transform cultural material in their writing has been studied in depth elsewhere (see for example Dyson 2003). Lévi-Strauss's notion of the *bricoleur* – one who appropriates the materials that are ready-to-hand to construct something new – can be usefully applied to the act of writing (Lévi-Strauss 1966: 21). *Bricolage* to the extent that it involves selection, appropriation and transformation of material can be seen as an aspect of the *bricoleur's* identity (Jenkins 1992). In Figure 4.6 a character card shows bricolage in action. Introducing the virtual character of Zema involves the writer in creating a

Figure 4.6 The Mighty Handbag character card

cartoon-like visual image that seems to be a blend of Mickey Mouse and Chubakker, whereas the character's accessories include 'The Dagger of Doom', borrowed from the PlayStation game *Ratchet and Clank*, juxtaposing this with the 'Mighty Handbag' (reminiscent of the Teletubbies' Tinky Winky).

Another aspect of bricolage involves the creation of hybrid texts. In writing emails children regularly import different discursive fragments into their texts. In Figure 4.7, a boy and girl co-write in response to a message from me. Having been away from my desk (real world identity), I have emailed to say that my virtual identity has been 'wrestling with the powers of darkness' (projective identity). This is the response (I am the eponymous owl) which is divided into sections A, B and C for ease of analysis.

Here, Section A is a direct response to my difficulties in 'wrestling with the powers of darkness'. 'Tips for you, owl' draws from two sources in children's popular culture – the genre of Pokemon cards (the reference to 'special attack') and that of console games (one of the correspondents being very familiar with *Tomb Raider* and the *Lord of the Rings* tie-in game). The section ends with the capitalised 'YOU NEED TO CHILL OUT' – interesting in that it uses a popular expression from youth culture. There is a topic change in the second section, as the two writers turn their attention to the adventure narrative. Events are

---

A.
Tips for you, owl
1: Use your head. Whats your special attack? Use it!
2: Send in reinforcements. You can't handle it all on your own.
3: Know who your dealing with. Don't just think they are just like a frendly postman.

There just tips that I had in mind and had to tell you. YOU NEED TO CHILL OUT, OWL.
B.
The crown is safe where it is. Somebody has found the crown. Dunno who he is like, but I trust this stanger. I'm only joking. The crown has been found and we will pick it up on our jorney. Don't send help. Pleeeeeeeeeeeese.
C.
The jorney should have already begun but Flint went to Cyprus and I lost my eye liner.
My lost eye liner was not found but we're gunna get some when we stop at Medowhall.

Got to fly, I've got an impatient taxi driver waiting. By the way, I saw a barn owl carreing a message yesterday, Was that you?

From

Robina & Flint.

Figure 4.7 Eyeliner email

reported, but this is done in an informal and almost casual manner amplified by the use of the conversational aside: 'Dunno who he is like.' This section concludes with 'please' which uses vowel reduplication for emphasis.

In Section C there is a change of direction: the topic of the journey now seems to refer to the ongoing narrative composition, as we encounter the real world identities of 'Robina' and 'Flint'. Robina needs more make-up from the shopping centre and Flint has just been on holiday to Cyprus. The message ends enigmatically. The two suggest that they are going to the shopping centre by taxi – this is not possible, after all they are at school – and we, as readers, begin to realise that we have entered another level of fiction. These writers have, in fact, created a multilayered narrative populated by their different identities.

From other projects there is similar evidence of borrowing. Here I trace one young writer's use of the red rose motif. Early emails regularly refer to the magical manifestation of red roses (Figure 4.8).

> To L,
> The strange things going on are that a couple of days ago I went to play in my garden, and all my flowers weren't there (as it is winter) but strangely there was a red rose standing there in the bare grass. I though this was strange but I just ignored it. But the next day I saw another red rose in the park with my friend on the bare grass, I told her but she thinks im looney. I feel like this thing is trying to tell me something. from kavita

Figure 4.8   Red rose email

She then becomes keen to produce an image of this rose which stands there 'in the bare grass' even though it is winter. Eventually, using a drawing programme she comes up with a graphic image complete with the verbal commentary 'Very weird!!' which is sent as an attachment (see Figure 4.9).

Figure 4.9   Very weird red rose attachment

The culmination of this girl's myth narrative shows how she borrows from various sources in her on-screen writing. The extract in Figure 4.10 shows the story opening in which she creates a bricolage of textual fragments while at the same time showing an awareness of the visual affordances of the screen. Her opening sentence contains three elements:

1 'There was once' is a common variation on the classic fairy-tale opening of 'once upon a time'.

2 'formally known as' reminds us of the tag of the pop icon 'the artist formerly known as Prince'.

3 'the hit Disney film Beauty and the Beast' uses the language of the film industry.

Here she shows herself to be an accomplished bricoleur. This is a multisemiotic text which uses the visual dimension of on-screen writing in the deployment of layout and colour. The original piece of writing uses a red font on a green background and is centre-justified. This is more than simple experimentation with word-processing tools; the writer is consciously using the red to represent the rose standing out against the green (grassy) background. In short she uses the visual and the verbal, and is clearly aware of how her writing looks on screen.

> There was once a beauty and a beast formally known as the hit Disney film Beauty and the Beast. The magic rose has reminded me of my great, great, great Grandma's death, as we had a familiar Rose lay on her chest.
> One night, I thought about it, but something was distracting me; it was some banging on my window. I drew the curtains nervously back but there was nothing there. But then something caught my eye; it was a big rapid scrape on my window.

Figure 4.10 Extract from Kavita's story

Discussion

Many of the texts that these projects generated show children recruiting different parts of their multilayered identities into the texts they produce. While some aspects of their writing are characteristic of the enclosures of bookspace, the electronic communication often seems more diverse, showing fluid movement between different facets of the writers' lifeworlds. Several commentators suggest that the act of presenting oneself, of exploring identity, is more salient in the composition of digital texts. Turkle's book is a treatise on this theme (Turkle 1995);

Lankshear, Peters and Knobel (1996) suggest that cyberspace presents 'extensive possibilities for constructing personal identity' (p.175); and Nakamura (2001) illustrates this in the context of Internet chatspaces.

The children involved in the projects described here used a variety of devices for presenting themselves both as actual and virtual characters. This analysis has shown how children introduce themselves through their writing, how they signal identity in their online communication and how they act as bricoleurs, borrowing discursive fragments from popular culture. This is not an exhaustive list, but serves to illustrate how they can develop agency through extended writing involving electronic communication. They become involved in an act of authorship. Holland *et al.* (1998) describe this in the following way:

> . . . the author, in everyday life as in artistic work, creates by orchestration, by arranging overheard elements, themes, and forms, not by some outpouring of an ineffable source. That is, the author works within, or at least against, a set of constraints that are also a set of possibilities for utterances.
>
> (Holland *et al.* 1998: 171)

And so the work described here perhaps goes some way to suggest the sorts of ' "awareness" and dispositions on the part of classroom learning communities' that were referred to in the introduction (Lankshear, Peters & Knobel 1996: 181). Certainly it seems feasible that an 'open-ended' project approach which includes the exchange of digital text introduces new textual possibilities as well as new ways of working. Young writers and interested educators can then begin to inhabit new spaces. Foucault argues that 'space is fundamental in any exercise of power'; this is true of the enclosures of bookspace that currently dominate literacy curricula. But he goes on to introduce the notion of *heterotopias* defined as 'those singular spaces to be found in some given social spaces whose functions are different or even the opposite of others' (quoted in Rainbow 1984: 252). At this point in time, digital text occupies this kind of space in educational practice but there is an urgent need for change, for as Dyson reminds us:

> In order to learn, children must be engaged in making sense of new information, new symbolic tools, and new ways of organizing, communicating, and taking action in the world around them. And this kind of human agency is generated by, and becomes meaningful within, a community with expectations for participation and production.
>
> (Dyson 2003: 76)

Digital media and the new forms of communication provide rich possibilities for redefining interaction, and establishing kinds of participation and production that reach out beyond classroom spaces – if we can imagine all that stuff really happening.

Implications for practice

In beginning to think more systematically about screen-based technology and the emergence of new ways of writing and communicating meaning, it is perhaps inevitable that we will reflect on the ways in which education presents and packages ICT. The work described in this chapter has been informed by a view that on-screen communication is really quite an ordinary, everyday practice which many children are already familiar with. Building on this, I suggest that we should:

● **Encourage children to experiment with writing using computers**

Writing on screen need not be a highly technical operation solely dependent on the mastery of difficult, specialist skills; rather it can be a tool to be used creatively, one that can open up new opportunities and new kinds of interaction. Incorporating new technology into the literacy curriculum is a form of enrichment, a way of building on the existing print-based practices of bookspace and anticipating the post-typographic practices of cyberspace.

● **Provide opportunities to use email for varied purposes in the classroom**

Email is now quite an established communicative medium and as schools develop a greater capacity for using digital communication it is important to document uses which provide alternatives to electronic pen-pals and online book discussions, whatever the merits of these. The opportunity for developing a sense of audience and purpose that email provides is likely to play an increasingly important role in our literacy curriculum – the examples provided here only begin to scratch the surface.

● **Value and celebrate children's production of multimodal texts**

Children's meaning-making could be typified as an exploration of multimodality. As Kress's work (e.g. Kress 2003) underlines, the screen provides new possibilities for communication. The interplay between the visual and the verbal is of particular interest in the work I have described. Children's imaginations appear to feed on what they have seen on screen and in the printed word and they fluently reframe this in the narratives they produce. Giving permission for this sort of work is not only motivating for children but also seems to enrich the quality of what they produce.

Supporting developing writers is partly about encouraging them to find a voice, to explore the power and practical significance of writing. Perhaps all successful writing teaching is about this sort of empowerment – about finding a voice. Using new technology can help young writers to develop their identity-in-writing as well as their identity-as-writers. Partly because of the close links between new technology and popular culture, new ways of writing seem to be able to help children to draw on their own lifeworlds and to bring material across the borders of their life in school and their life outside school.

References

Bakhtin, M. (1981) 'Discourse in the Novel', in C. Emerson & M. Holquist (eds) *The Dialogic Imagination: Four Essays by M. Bakhtin*. Austin: University of Texas.

Clay, M. (1975) *What did I write?* Auckland, New Zealand: Heinemann Educational Books.

Crystal, D. (2001) *Language and the Internet*. Cambridge: Cambridge University Press.

de Pourbaix, R. (2000) 'Literacy in an Electronic Community', in D. Barton, M. Hamilton & R. Ivanic (eds) *Situated Literacies – Reading and Writing in Context*. London: Routledge.

Dyson, A. H. (1997) *Writing Superheroes – Contemporary Childhood, Popular Culture and Classroom Literacy*. New York: Teachers College Press.

Dyson, A. H. (2003) *The Brothers and the Sisters Learn to Write*. New York: Teachers College Press.

Foucault, M. (1977) *Discipline and Punish – The Birth of the Prison*. Harmondsworth: Penguin.

Halliday, M. A. K. (1978) *Language as Social Semiotic: the Social Interpretation of Language and Meaning*. London: Edward Arnold.

Harpin, W. (1976) *The Second 'R' – Writing Development in the Junior School*. London: Allen and Unwin.

Holland, D., Lachicotte, W., Skinner, D. & Cain, C. (1998) *Identity and Agency in Cultural Worlds*. Cambridge, MA: Harvard University Press.

Holloway, S. & Valentine, G. (2002) *Cyberkids: Youth Identities and Communities in an On-line World*. London: RoutledgeFalmer.

Hull, G. & Schultz, K. (2001) 'Literacy and Learning Out of School: A Review of Theory and Research', *Review of Educational Research*, 71(4), 575–611.

Jenkins, H. (1992) *Textual Poachers: Television Fans and Participatory Culture*. London: Routledge.

Kress, G. (2003) *Literacy in the New Media Age*. London: Routledge.

Lankshear, C., Peters, M. & Knobel, M. (1996) 'Critical Pedagogy and Cyberspace', in H.A. Giroux, C. Lankshear, P. McLaren & M. Peters (eds) *Counternarratives: Cultural Studies and Critical Pedagogies in Postmodern Spaces*. London: Routledge.

Lévi-Strauss, C. (1966) *The Savage Mind*. Chicago: University of Chicago Press.

Merchant, G. (2003) 'E-mail Me Your Thoughts: Digital Communication and Narrative Writing', *Reading, Literacy and Language*, 37(3).

Nakamura, L. (2001) 'The Race In/For Cyberspace: Identity Tourism and Racial Passing on the Internet', in D. Trend (ed.) *Reading Digital Culture*. Oxford: Blackwell.

Peters, M. & Lankshear, C. (1996) 'Postmodern Counternarratives', in H.A. Giroux, C. Lankshear, P. McLaren & M. Peters (eds) *Counternarratives: Cultural Studies and Critical Pedagogies in Postmodern Spaces*. London: Routledge.

Rainbow, P. (ed.) (1984) *The Foucault Reader*. Toronto: Random House.

Turkle, S. (1995) *Life on the Screen: Identity in the Age of the Internet*. New York: Simon and Schuster.

Wenger, E. (1998) *Communities of Practice – Learning, Meaning and Identity*. Cambridge: CUP.

PART 2

Focusing on texts with a critical eye: Critical literacy in the primary school

Literacy is never neutral. All texts contain particular views of the world along with associated attitudes and values. This section looks at children who, in partnership with their teachers, are interacting with and responding to texts and popular culture icons in critical, socially perceptive ways and who are being encouraged to take social action in relation to the issues they are considering.

Creating opportunities for critical literacy with young children
Using everyday issues and everyday text

Vivian Vasquez

This chapter highlights opportunities for engaging pleasurable and powerful critical literacies by looking closely at four- to seven-year-old children's appropriations of everyday texts and the social issues that stem from those texts. Some children from Canada and the USA were part of a three-year study linking literacy development with everyday texts. Specifically, I will demonstrate the integration of critical literacies in curricula for young children through the use of texts such as food wrappers and toy packaging. Ways that children participate in various forms of text analysis will be shown along with the children's re-design of these texts.

> A critical literacy curriculum needs to be lived. It arises from the social and political conditions that unfold in communities in which we live. As such it cannot be traditionally taught. In other words, as teachers we need to incorporate a critical perspective into our everyday lives with the children we work with in order to find ways to help them understand the social and political issues around them.
>
> (Vasquez 2004a)

In this chapter my intent is to show and tell about creating spaces for engaging in 'pleasurable and powerful critical literacies' (Comber 2000) with young children using various texts and issues of everyday life. Comber (2000) describes critical literacies as involving people using language to exercise power, to enhance everyday life in schools and communities, and to question practices of privilege and injustice. Throughout the chapter you will meet children between the ages of four and seven who have participated in doing the kind of critical work that Comber describes.

I will begin by providing a brief overview of what it means to negotiate spaces for critical literacies through the use of everyday issues and text. Following this, I show and tell what happens when the official and unofficial worlds of school intersect by describing work done on buying, selling and advertising by a seven-year-old boy called Miles. I will then share other opportunities for creating spaces for critical literacies through the use of magazine ads, toy packaging and other popular culture artefacts. I conclude by sharing important questions teachers ought to consider to integrate critical literacies in their own settings and contexts.

Building curriculum from the issues and texts of everyday life

My experience working with teachers attempting to engage in critical literacy shows in many cases social issues, i.e. racism, classism, gender equity, are treated as variables to be added to the existing curriculum. This, rather than using these issues to build curriculum, is done because the topics are associated with cynicism and un-pleasurable work, the kind of work that 'steals childhood away from children'. However, critical literacy does not necessarily involve taking a negative stance, rather it includes looking at an issue or topic in different ways, analysing it and hopefully being able to suggest possibilities for change or improvement.in ways that are both challenging and enjoyable (Vasquez 2004b). Often socially charged issues such as disadvantage or racism seem to be looked upon as heavy-handed issues. The discussions I have had with children I have taught and those who have participated in my research, along with the work we accomplished, were very pleasurable, involving both seriousness and enjoyment. We approached our work with zest because the topics that we dealt with were socially significant to us. They were issues that mattered in our daily lives and with which we were passionately familiar.

In a study on the links between everyday popular culture and language arts instruction, Alvermann and Hong Xu (2003) note four approaches in particular to using popular culture in the classroom: pop-culture as detrimental to children's development, teaching children to critically analyse popular culture texts, emphasising the pleasure children take in various forms of media-produced text, and developing their ability to be self-reflexive in their uses of popular culture. They state what they feel is problematic with some of these approaches, affirming their endorsement of the fourth approach, developing children's ability to be self-reflexive in their uses of popular culture as an effective way of engaging with popular culture texts. They define self-reflexivity within the context of working with popular culture texts as a way of 'striking a balance between teaching [children] to be critical and allowing them to experience pleasures without challenges that can extend their learning' (p. 148).

The question for me is, how can we strike a balance between creating spaces or opportunities for childhood popular culture discourses and everyday texts in the classroom and engage children in working critically with these texts while at the same time making sure not to co-opt their interests. Co-opting their interests refers to taking over such things as popular culture texts about which the children are passionate and turning them into school curriculum thereby making those texts less desirable. Striking this balance calls for ongoing negotiation of curriculum with children and ongoing observations of what everyday issues and texts are on the minds of children. This negotiation involves constantly listening to what children are talking about, their passions, their interests and using these to build curriculum. There are increasing accounts of such work with children of all ages (Alverman & Hong Xu 2003; Comber 1993; Dyson 2003; O'Brien 1998; Luke, O'Brien & Comber 1994; Vasquez 2004a; in press).

Everyday texts: What are they?

When I use the term 'everyday texts' I am referring to texts that are spoken or written as part of everyday life, such as newspaper and magazine ads, food wrappers or television advertisements. 'These texts can be so common that we do not carefully take notice of them. As a result we can be less aware of the kinds of messages about our world, which they convey' (Vasquez in press). Since these texts are not natural representations of the world they can be interrogated, deconstructed and analysed to uncover the view of the world they represent. In doing so we are able to make visible the lifestyles and social identities that are constructed through what is presented and how it is presented.

Connections and mismatches between the everyday world and the official classroom curriculum

I met seven-year-old Miles while observing a pre-service teacher present a lesson on categorisation, sorting and classifying in a classroom for seven- and eight-year-olds. In the United States pre-service teachers are college students who are simultaneously taking courses in a school of education for the purposes of teacher certification while also spending time in a classroom setting. Vickie, the pre-service teacher I was observing, used insects as the theme for doing this work. She had cut out dozens of images of insects, which she mounted on 5×5cm pieces of cardboard. The back of each card was labelled with the insect's name. The children were assigned to small groups. Each group was given a bag filled with approximately 20 insect cards. Vickie asked each group member to take on a particular responsibility such as being a recorder, spokesperson or timer. She then asked the children to think of different categories in which they could sort their insect cards such as winged, jumping, furry, colourful and crawling. It was while the 'official' categorisation of insects curriculum was taking place that Miles began a conversation with me.

Miles: Who are you again? What's your name, a doctor right?
Vivian: Vivian Vasquez.

Miles: Should I call you Vivian (tilts his head down and peeks in the direction where his teacher is sitting) or Dr Vasquez?

Vivian: What are you more comfortable calling me? What should I call you?

Miles: I'm Miles. Better call you Dr Vasquez. Do you like art?

Vivian: Definitely.

Miles: Let me show you some.

With this Miles left, momentarily returning with a 'How to Draw' book, which showed step-by-step instructions on how to draw a number of different images of animals and other creatures. He began flipping the pages of the book pointing at each image and nodding his head softly saying, 'nice drawings, huh?' and as if to insinuate that having one of these images is desirable. As I looked more carefully through the book I noticed that each image had a price tag directly below it. For example, some had 22 cents, 25 cents or 27 cents printed in pencil.

'What are these?' I asked, pointing to the price tag on one of the pages in the book. Miles replied, 'Well, you see that guy over there?' He was pointing out another child in the class. 'His name is Kyle. He's an artist. He draws the pictures. I'm his business manager so I get him jobs,' Miles continued. At this point, the classroom teacher noticed that Miles was not at his desk, at which time he was told to get back on task. Within minutes he had completed what he had been asked to do and was once again standing beside the table where I sat. 'Anyhow,' Miles picked up from our previous talk as though he had never left, 'I'm Kyle's business manager. Antwan is his consultant' (pointing out another child in the classroom). Miles explained that the main job of a consultant is to help the artist decide what drawings people will want to buy. After I asked him how Antwan knew what people would buy, Miles told me that he and Antwan had done a survey in the schoolyard to see which kinds of drawings children would like best. 'One of these can be yours if you like,' he continued. 'Which one do you like anyhow?' he asked. I flipped through the book and told him I liked the dragon image best of all.

Miles: Are you sure you wouldn't rather have the gryphon?
            (The dragon was priced at 22 cents plus tax.)
            It's only 27 cents including tax. And (dramatic pause) free delivery. (Laughing) Well, it'll only be from that side of the room to this side of the room.

Vivian: Including tax. What's the base price?

Miles: (Looks at a price list he had created of base prices and the corresponding tax.) Twenty-six cents plus 5 per cent tax is about 27 cents total.

Vivian: But I like the dragon.

Miles: Okay then. Last chance to change your mind. Okay. That one's only 22 cents tax included.

Having sealed our deal, Miles left my side to place an order for a dragon drawing with Kyle, the artist. A little later Miles came back to where I was sitting to deliver my purchase and a receipt (see Figures 5.1a and 5.1b).

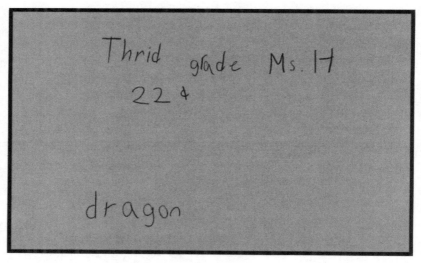

Figure 5.1a   Purchase receipt

Figure 5.1b   Drawing of the dragon

Connections between the official curriculum and Miles' unofficial literacies

There are obvious connections between the official school curriculum and Miles' unofficial work. For example, the lesson during which Miles engaged in his business transaction dealt with the skill of sorting things into categories based on particular attributes. While deciding on how to price the drawings, Miles and his friends sorted the images into three price categories depending on how complex they were to draw. They also took a survey in the schoolyard to see which drawings children liked best. In the official curriculum the teacher gave each child a particular role to play in their small groups. For example, each small group had a recorder, timer and spokesperson. Miles, Kyle and Antwan also took on individual roles and responsibilities as Business Manager, Artist and Consultant.

The spaces where the official curriculum and the unofficial work overlap are particularly important for those attempting to engage in critical literacies but who feel the pressures of being accountable for 'covering' the mandated curriculum. What will become evident later in this chapter is the way in which Miles' unofficial schoolwork provided spaces for him to develop literacy skills beyond that which was mandated for children his age by the school board. As such his unofficial work provided him with opportunities to develop literacy skills that carry status or capital within and beyond the official curriculum.

My interest with Miles' work, however, goes beyond an interest in looking at the connections between the official and unofficial curriculum. I am interested in the possibilities that capitalising on his work has for engaging in a critical literacy curriculum. I am also interested in uncovering the privileging of particular literacies over everyday literacies.

Dyson (1993) discusses the notion of a 'permeable curriculum' as a way of using what children know as a bridge that gives them access to what will bring them capital in the world. For example, how might the literacies that Miles, Kyle and Antwan bring to the classroom be used as a bridge to help children learn about the relationship between language and power? While talking about critical language awareness, Hilary Janks (1993) states:

> When people use language to speak or write, they have to make many choices. They have to decide what words to use, whether to include adjectives and adverbs, whether to use the present, the past or the future, whether to use sexist or non-sexist pronouns, whether to join sentences or to leave them separate, how to sequence information, whether to be definite or tentative, approving or disapproving. What all these choices mean is that written and spoken texts are constructed from a range of possible language options.

> (p. iii)

How then can we create a meaningful curriculum by capitalising on the literacies brought to school by Miles and his friends in order to make visible a range of possible language options as a way of giving children an opportunity to become critical readers of the word and the world (Freire 1987)?

A closer look at Miles' language options

A closer look at Miles' language options and the words he chooses to use during his conversation with me brings to the fore his literacy strengths. When Miles asks,

'Who are you again? What's your name, a doctor right?' he takes on a similar role as both an advertising agent and a seller of goods (drawings in particular). He uses questioning, 'Who are you again?' and 'What's your name . . .?' to make it clear to me that he was interested in striking up a conversation with me. By asking if I was a doctor, he made it obvious that he knew something already about me. He was a step ahead in our conversation. This was a good strategy for someone soon to put on his hat as a salesperson. He kept me in the conversation by continuing to pay attention to me when he asked, 'Should I call you Vivian or Dr Vasquez?' This added a personal layer to our talk. Knowing each other's names allowed us to use our names to refer to one another. He then introduced me to his product by asking, 'Do you like art?' My response, 'definitely', is the hook he used to continue with the task he had set for himself, to sell me a drawing.

Miles' comment, 'nice drawings, huh?', said while nodding his head up and down, affected me as buyer by leading me to the response he desired, 'yes'. He used this positive statement along with another statement, 'one of these can be yours if you like', to create certainty for me, his potential buyer (Granville 1993). His next question, 'Which one do you like anyway?' is loaded because of its underlying message, which was, 'you want a drawing, and you just don't know which one yet.' He continued to hone his skills at being a good seller when he asked, 'Are you sure you wouldn't rather have the gryphon?' and when he made the statement, 'It's only 27 cents including tax', in an attempt to get me to purchase a more expensive drawing. He was also teaching me to be a particular kind of buyer or consumer by enticing me with an offer of 'free delivery included' if I were to immediately act on his offer. When he says, 'Last chance to change your mind', referring to my decision to buy the drawing of a dragon, he casts doubt on my purchase choice in the hope that I would change my mind to buy the more expensive gryphon.

How does the story of Miles connect with critical literacy and new times?

According to Luke (1998), new literacies refer to new times and places where learners acquire literacy. Phil Cormack (2000) talks about new times as what is happening *now*. I wanted to begin this chapter with the story of Miles to start a discussion about how schools can recognise, capitalise and act on the different literacies appropriated by children in the everyday world, often outside of school. These literacies come in many different forms and stem from a multiplicity of contexts. Miles' story allows me to make visible the sorts of literacies that could emerge in classrooms if we start to negotiate opportunities for engaging with everyday texts and stop privileging traditional print-based texts. In the rest of this chapter I will focus on other contexts for taking up critical literacies using popular culture texts such as toy packaging and magazine ads.

Using toy packaging to engage in critical language awareness

Taylor: I'm opening my next pack . . . I got a Gengar Holo, Japanese. Ummm, have, have, have, don't have, don't have, don't have . . . don't have! Wow! These cards, these packs are really starting to pay off!

Vivian: Why do you say that?

Taylor: Because I don't really, I don't, I don't have most of the cards that are in the pack! (loud gasp) I got a (pause) holo! Don't have, don't have, don't have, don't have, have, don't have, don't have. Wow! I wasn't joking when I said these are starting to pay off! I'm opening one more pack. Show me the money! Wow! I hardly have any of these cards here! Holy tamale!

The previous exchange was part of a conversation I had with six-year-old Taylor as he opened packages of Pokemon cards. Pokemon is a name given to a popular series of what are called 'pocket monsters', imaginary characters that have various capabilities such as being able to transform into different versions of the same character, and powers, such as using water, electricity or fire to fend off opponents. These characters live in an alternate reality where they have the ability to evolve by winning battles over one another (Vasquez 2003).

The term 'holo' which Taylor used in describing one of his cards was short for holographic, or in this case holographic Pokemon cards, a limited number of which were randomly included in the card packs. To open a Pokemon package and find a holo is therefore very desirable, explaining Taylor's excitement when he said, 'Wow! These cards, these packs are really starting to pay off!' Here he was re- ferring to the money he spent buying the cards as paying off because the potential value of the new cards exceeded the money he paid for the pack. He proved this interpretation to be accurate when he said 'I'm opening one more pack. Show me the money!' According to Luke (1997), although children are not direct income earners, they exert significant power over parental purchase choices. It is no sur- prise therefore to find children like Taylor who are able to participate in the world of Pokemon by having available to them opportunities to access and purchase various Pokemon products. The fact that children do exert significant purchasing power makes it even more important for educators to find ways to negotiate the use of everyday texts in the classroom.

Later in our conversation, Taylor explained that holos are somewhat rare, that is they are not in very many card packs, and so they are worth more in the trading card world. They are worth a good amount of money. Also worth a good amount of status in the world of Pokemon are complete sets of cards. When Taylor said, 'have, have, don't have, don't have, don't have . . . don't have!' he was going through his new packs of cards verbalising which of the cards in the pack he already had and which ones he did not have. This is the same routine that takes place during card trading when traders look through each other's cards prior to negotiating a trade.

Over the years Pokemon has become a hot topic of conversation for both children and adults. Children have developed various discursive practices specific to being part of the Pokemon gaming world, for example, Taylor's use of the word 'holo' which makes sense to other Pokemon traders. Adults, on the other hand, have engaged in conversation about these pocket monsters primarily to scrutinise their potential to encourage violent behaviour in children. In fact in autumn 2000 even John Stossel, a well-known television reporter in the USA, dedicated an entire news segment to Pokemon, whereby he balked at those who claim that participating with this popular culture text encourages kids to gamble because a large part of the Pokemon world has to do with trading cards. Pokemon have even had a turn at being on the cover of *Time* magazine (1999). Pikachu, one of the most known Pokemon characters, was included in the famous Thanksgiving Day Macy's Parade joining the ranks of Snoopy and Curious George in an American tradition that started in 1927. There have even been entire conferences dedicated to the study of Pokemon as a new times phenomenon. One such conference was held at the University of Hawaii Center for Japanese Studies Endowment, in November 2000. The conference involved an international team of professors, lecturers and media scholars from around the world who gathered to discuss the phenomenon. It has become truly phenomenal to see the diverse array of goods available for anyone interested in Pokemon, including videotapes of the television cartoons, full-length animated movies, lunch boxes, clothing, toys, bedding, shoes, bags and backpacks, towels, books and other school supplies. Pokemon has become such a hot popular culture commodity that large corporations have thrown their brand names into the mix, making available such food items as Kraft Pokemon Macaroni and Cheese™ and Kellogg's Pokemon Cereal™. This branding and mass-producing of Pokemon-related items results in:

- the creation of a lasting engagement with the Pokemon audience;
- providing for the 'sellers' (companies that produce Pokemon products) a deep well of marketing and advertising possibilities;
- providing for the sellers shared cultural images that already exist in people's minds thus making their products more recognisable and therefore desirable.

Historically, Pokemon took its place as a mega hit television cartoon in 1998 when the cartoon first aired and children were introduced to the Pokemon theme song and the phrase 'Gotta Catch 'Em All', the Pokemon mantra. (For a historical overview of Pokemon go to http://www.genting.com.my/en/retailers/fwplaza/pokemon02.htm.) The catchphrase became so well known by children of all ages that in any classroom I visited during the time of this research in both Canada and the United States, when I asked children what 'Gotta Catch 'Em All' referred to they immediately responded, 'Pokemon!' In the previous transcript of my talk with Taylor, his verbally labelling each card as either one he had or did not have was all part of the collecting behaviour stemming from the desire to 'catch 'em all', that is to collect as comprehensive a card collection as possible.

While looking across a series of Pokemon toy packages for the purposes of working on some critical language awareness on how audience is maintained, the following conversation took place.

Curtis: You can find 'Gotta Catch 'Em All' in almost all the posters that you find.
Vivian: Any ideas why that might be?
Curtis: Uh, I don't know. I can take a guess though.
Vivian: Okay.
Curtis: Well, in the show, the object is to catch all the Pokemon. So maybe that 'Gotta Catch 'Em All' means you gotta (pause) catch them all.
Vivian: So catching, is that the same as or different than collecting?
Emily: It's sort of like collecting cards.
Miguel: Except you're collecting the Pokemon.
Emily: Who wants us to do that?
Miguel: The sellers?
Curtis: Ya, they make the Pokemon for their job.

Like Miles in the opening of this chapter, the four- to six-year-old children who participated in this conversation raised important issues regarding 'sellers', 'buyers' and the consumer world. Janet Evans' chapter in this book looks in more detail at some older children's perceptions of these issues in relation to Beanie Babies. In another publication (Vasquez 2004b), I did a closer analysis of the conversation that followed this previous exchange whereby I asked the children to look across a series of Pokemon toy packages to find all the words that have to do with collecting. I concluded that it was conversations like this one that set the groundwork for later conversations whereby the children and I began to look more closely at the use of words linked to Pokemon texts and how these ideologically positioned readers; that is, how the texts reflect dominant social ideas or beliefs. We did an analysis of the texts by bringing to the fore the way that audience is maintained through the consistent use of the phrase 'Gotta Catch 'Em All'. As Curtis states, 'in almost all the posters (referring to toy packaging, posters, magazines and other Pokemon-related products) you find'. We also brought to the fore the notion of consumerism when Emily asked, 'Who wants us to do that?' and Miguel replied, 'The sellers'. We also discovered that the same collecting behaviour was encouraged with food items such as Kraft Pokemon Macaroni and Cheese, and Kellogg's Pokemon Cereal. Regarding the macaroni and cheese, for instance, four-year-old Emily noted, 'Instead you don't say catch. It's eat. You "Gotta Eat 'Em All".' In the same vein Rula noted, 'Like for clothes. You gotta wear them all' referring to the various clothing items that were being manufactured bearing Pokemon characters. Rula's comment regarding clothing led us to further analysis of Pokemon texts, this time with an eye towards constructions of gender.

The children's constructions of gender

Rula: Do you have clothes that are Pokemon?

Miguel: Nah, I don't wear girl stuff, that's gross.

Emily: You have shoes!

Miguel: Shoes aren't clothes, they're just shoes.

Rula: Why? Are clothes girls only?

Miguel: I mean like a pink shirt with Pikachu or something.

Regardless of what Emily and Rula said, Miguel was convinced that Pokemon clothes were for girls only and that Pokemon shoes were for boys. According to its creators Pokemon are non-gendered and as such they should have equal appeal to girls and boys. However, in conversation with the children it is clear that this is not the case. In order to push the discussion further I asked the children if they would be interested in designing their own shirts and shoes. The following day I had prepared sheets of paper with blank T-shirts and shoes to use as templates for their designs. Five-year-old Patrick designed the shirt in Figure 5.2 as a shirt that would most appeal to boys. He said this would be a boy shirt because he drew a Pokemon that boys like with all the powers that it has (referring to the symbols in the circles across the shoulders of the shirt). After seeing many other such designs from some

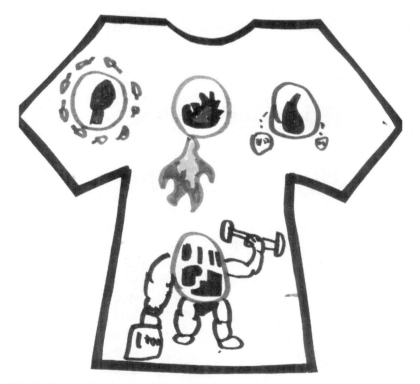

Figure 5.2   T-shirt design that would appeal to boys

Figure 5.3　Design for a shoe logo that would appeal to girls

of the other children, Miguel seemed satisfied that boys could wear Pokemon clothing also. He said, 'That's funny, I didn't think you could do that. Doh.'

Six-year-old Catalina designed the logo to go on a girl's shoe that is seen in Figure 5.3. The logo is a purple unicorn-looking animal with a flowing blonde mane. She called the Pokemon logo that she designed 'Colours' and said that it is a horse-type Pokemon. She decided to add to her design a write-up of the Pokemon saying that her mother's shoes came with a paper about the shoes. She attributes several attacks to Colours: star attack, head butt, yellow attack, shield attack and colour attack. Attacks are basically a Pokemon's weapons, the ways in which it can beat an opponent in battle. Her write-up, which can be seen in Figure 5.4, was done in a shoe outline. She notes that this Pokemon is very rare and that he can take away other Pokemon's power. She continues by writing, 'He has no weakness. This Pokemon is very strong and big. This Pokemon can fly very fast. It always has good ideas.'

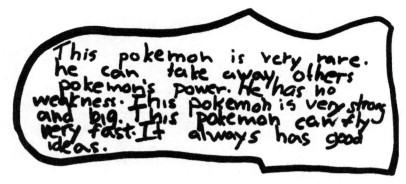

This pokemon is very rare. he can take away others pokemon's power. He has no weakness. This pokemon is very strong and big. This pokemon can fly very fast. It always has good ideas.

Figure 5.4 Shoe write-up

Re-design as a crucial element in critical literacy

Janks (2002) talks about redesign as an element that should be part of any critical literacy work that we do. In our conversation regarding gender, simply deconstructing gendered texts such as T-shirts and shoes would not have been enough to offer the children an alternate perspective. Clearly, especially for Miguel, it was not until we designed our own versions of Pokemon shoes and shirts that he realised other alternatives existed, bringing to the fore the notion that texts and images are socially constructed and as such they can be deconstructed and re-designed. His statement, 'That's funny, I didn't think you could do that. Doh', was his 'aha' moment, that is, his moment of suddenly realising things could be other than what he originally thought.

Catalina's re-design of a Pokemon shoe was especially interesting to me as she broke down gender stereotypes through her choice of text and image. She began by saying 'this Pokemon is very rare', immediately giving it added value as in the holo cards that Taylor mentioned earlier in the chapter. At another point in time the children and I had a discussion regarding which Pokemon they thought were male and which were female and why. What I discovered was that the children looked primarily at the characters' physical attributes to decide on maleness or femaleness. What a character did not look like, e.g. the lack of boy colours such as blue or green, was also a criterion used to assign gender. Most of the Pokemon that the children claimed to be female were not as powerful or valuable as some of the Pokemon the children claimed to be male. So to say that Colours, who to the other children looked female, was very rare and therefore very valuable disrupted the schema they had earlier developed for assigning gender. This disruption continued as Catalina wrote that Colours 'can take away other Pokemon's power' and that 'he has no weakness'. Colours, originally thought to be a female by the children, was in fact male according to Catalina. The other children had fully expected, given the way the unicorn looked, that it would be a female, especially since it resembled Lila Unicorn from Barbie of Swan Lake, a popular toy with the girls.

When I asked her why she decided to create a 'female'-looking male Pokemon, she basically said that it was because there are lots of ways that males look and lots of ways that females look and that people should not just use how someone looks on the outside to decide what they are really like. She explained, 'Just because a boy likes pink it doesn't mean he isn't strong or just because a girl likes blue it doesn't mean she'll beat up other kids.'

She continues to add value to Colours the Pokemon by continuing to describe his strength, saying that he is not only strong but very strong and big too. To put icing on the cake, she finishes off by saying that 'this Pokemon can fly very fast and it always has good ideas'.

What we accomplished therefore was to use the principle of re-designing to challenge dominant meanings (Janks 1993) which was one way to help the children to begin to understand that 'texts are constructed from a range of possible options' (p. iii).

Analysing the visual grammar of advertisements

After having engaged in designing Pokemon artefacts such as shirts and shoes, the children and I began talking about what it would mean to sell those products. What would cause someone to want to buy something? What kinds of images would be effective? What words sound most convincing? How do the texts and images in advertising work? How can we read these texts with a critical eye so that we are able to make informed decisions about what we buy?

In this section I will focus on the technical characteristics of visual images, their social functions, the context of text images and what this type of analysis might look like in classrooms.

The concept of offer and demand

Halliday (1978) describes four basic functions of speech as *offering* information, *offering* goods and services, *demanding* information, and *demanding* goods and services. Kress and van Leeuwen (1996) have taken this concept of offer and demand and applied it to visual images.

One of the Pokemon artefacts brought to the classroom by the children was a *Kids Tribute* magazine, a publication dedicated to children about current movies for young people. One of the ads in the magazine particularly caught our attention because it took up two pages. On the right side a group of Pokemon are portrayed entering into some sort of arena or stadium. The image is similar to the entrance of players during professional sporting events such as basketball, football or hockey. The ad is for Pokemon Stadium, which is a video game. It is billed as 'the Pokemon battle you've been waiting for . . . the way Pokemon were meant to battle'.

In the ad, the people in the stands are made to appear as though they are cheering for the entering Pokemon in the same way that sports fans cheer for their favourite teams and players. Using this ad, one of the things that could be focused on is the relationship in Western society between power and being a professional athlete and how this is being connected to what it means to be a Pokemon trainer. For now, however, I would like to focus on the concept of 'offer and demand' as it pertains to this particular image.

Kress and van Leeuwen (1996: 122) talk about the fundamental difference between pictures where the participants in the image, the characters, in this case the Pokemon, look directly at the readers' eyes and pictures where this is not the case. They state 'when represented participants look directly at the viewer, vectors, formed by participants' eyelines, connect the participants with the viewer. Contact is established even if it is only on an imaginary level' (p.122).

Using Kress and van Leeuwen's strategy, I made an overhead of the double-page ad which I projected on the classroom wall. Together, the children and I drew lines, from each of the characters' eyes, enabling us to have a closer look at where the vectors formed by their eyelines would end. Having done this it was clear that the characters – Pikachu, Meowth, Psyduck, Poliwhirl, Venusaur, Blastoise and Charizard – gaze directly toward us, the viewers. One of the characters, Charizard, was positioned, in the ad, flying over the other Pokemon. This visual effect helps with the illusion that the Pokemon are coming towards the viewer, therefore maintaining the Pokemons' contact with the viewer.

Kress and van Leeuwen also state that there can be 'vectors, formed by a gesture in the same direction' (1996: 122). In the ad Pikachu, Meowth, Poliwhirl, Venusaur, Blastoise and Charizard all have one arm back and one arm with a forward vector. This is seen more clearly in an ad for Pokemon puzzles where Ash is holding a Pokeball directly at the viewer and even more clearly in a Super Mario figure located in the bottom left-hand corner on the left side of the double-page spread. This gesture is reminiscent of 'We Want You' US Armed Forces recruitment posters. The children and I looked at this gesture in a number of ads and also tried doing the gesture ourselves. We also then posed with our arms stretched out in different directions and talked about which ones most effectively made the viewers feel as though they were being asked to participate. Curtis even went as far as to create his own Pokemon stadium out of clay in order to play with the idea of gestures and how audience is constructed (Figure 5.5).

The configuration of the participants' gaze and hand gesture functions in particular ways. First, the visual formation used creates direct address; a 'visual you' is formed through this address, that is, an image design that indicates to the reader 'I am talking to you.' Secondly, the producer of the image uses it to do something to the viewer. As such Kress and van Leeuwen refer to this kind of image as a 'demand' (1996: 123). They state, 'the participants' gaze (and the gesture, if present) demands something from the viewer, demands that the viewer

Figure 5.5 Curtis' Pokemon Stadium in clay

enter into some kind of imaginary relation with him or her' (p.122). The image through the use of gaze and gesture signifies a 'hey you, I mean you, join me in battle, play with me buy me and you will be powerful too' kind of relationship. So when images 'demand', what they are demanding are the 'goods and services' that realise a particular social relation (Kress & van Leeuwen 1996: 129). In this case one relationship is that of producer and consumer. As such the visual image defines the viewer. What does this ad say I can and cannot be? What does this ad say I can and cannot do?

Conclusion

While thinking about my interactions with Miles at the start of this chapter, and the work that the children and I did using popular culture everyday texts alongside the work being done as the 'official curriculum' (the curriculum mandated by the school district), I began to consider ways of using the literacies appropriated by children in their everyday world as resources for creating curriculum. In doing so, a number of questions came to mind. They are:

- In classrooms, what discursive practices are assembled together to construct children as literate beings?

- What literacies dominate classrooms and how might other literacies be made available?

- How might a classroom curriculum look different if the literacies brought into the classroom by children like Miles, Kyle and Antwan are used to construct the curriculum?

- What are the literacies and/or resources that children bring into the classroom?

- Where did they appropriate these literacies? In other words, what are the places where these literacies were acquired and how?

- What literacies are privileged in classrooms? What literacies are ignored? How might we change what literacies are privileged?

- In what ways does working with everyday texts and issues create spaces for developing literacies that go well beyond that which is mandated in the official curriculum?

These questions may be challenging but they are important to consider if we are to effectively use everyday texts and issues to create spaces for critical literacy with young children. They enable us, as Luke (1998) suggests, not only to see how the world of texts works in ideological ways, but also to use texts as social tools in ways that allow for a reconstruction of inequitable worlds. What matters most, however, is that we get started doing some of this important life work, and it is life work because the kinds of literacies that stem from this work are the literacies of everyday life.

Implications for practice

● Start to look critically at popular culture artefacts as soon as possible

My suggestion would be to start where you can, as soon as you can. For instance, you could look at one aspect of toy packaging (the cardboard wrapping around toys or the boxes they come in) or a magazine ad. One of the toy packages we analysed had a gold seal in one corner that had on it, 'Increase your intelligence power!' A Pokemon Pop Tarts food package also had a gold seal in the upper right-hand corner. It said, 'Limited Edition'. A place to start could be to take a similar ad and focus specifically on the seal. When I did this analysis with children, I asked them who they thought would be interested in the words on the seal. Their responses are shown in Figure 5.6.

You could then have children brainstorm possible audiences and then create their own versions of the seal for those audiences (see Figures 5.7a and 5.7b). By doing these kinds of activities you can begin to create opportunities for looking at how texts are constructed and re-designing texts for particular audiences with an eye towards becoming critical readers of text.

● Pay close attention to opportunities to work critically with texts

Always keep in mind that a critical literacy curriculum needs to be lived. It arises from the social and political conditions that unfold in communities in which we

> Increase your
> Intelligence
> Power!
>
> - Teachers
>   Because they want [children] to learn.
>
> - Parents
>   Because they want their kids to be smart.
>
> - Principal
>   So the school will do good.
>
> - Collectors
>   So they can have a rare collection.
>
> - Kids
>   To be cool because maybe not everyone would have it.
>
> LIMITED
> EDITION
>
> - The guy at the trading card store
>   So he can sell it to someone else for lots of money.

Figure 5.6 Who would be interested in the words on the seal?

Figure 5.7(a) Examples of seals created by children   **Figure 5.7(b)**

live. As such it cannot be traditionally taught. In other words, as teachers we need to incorporate a critical perspective into our everyday lives with our children on an ongoing basis in order to find ways to help children understand the social and political issues around them (Vasquez 2004a).

- **Value and encourage children's use of multiple ways of knowing about texts**

Ensure that you provide children with opportunities to communicate their ideas in different ways including drawing and creating multimodal texts. Guy Merchant talks about this in detail in Chapter 4 in this book.

References

Alvermann, D.E. & Hong Xu, S. (2003) 'Children's Everyday Literacies: Intersections of Popular Culture and Language Arts Instruction', *Language Arts*, 81 (2), 145–54.

Comber, B. (1993) 'Classroom Explorations in Critical Literacy', *Australian Journal of Language and Literacy*, 16 (1), 73–83.

Comber, B. (2000) 'What Really Counts in Early Literacy Lessons', *Language Arts*, 78 (1), 39–49.

Cormack, P. (2000) 'Workshop Presentation, Mount Saint Vincent University', *International Literacy Educators Action Research Network*, Mississauga, Ontario.

Dyson, A.H. (1993) *Social Worlds of Children Learning to Write in an Urban Primary School*. New York: Teachers College Press.

Dyson, A.H. (2003) 'Popular Literacies and the "All" Children: Rethinking Literacy Development for Contemporary Childhoods', *Language Arts*, 81 (2), 100–109.

Freire, P. (1987) *Literacy: Reading the Word and the World*. Bergin and Garvey Publishers.

Granville, S. (1993) *Language, Advertising and Power*. London: Hodder and Stoughton.

Halliday, M.A.K. (1978) *Language as Social Semiotic*. London: Edward Arnold.

Janks, H. (1993) *Language, Identity, and Power*. London: Hodder and Stoughton.

Janks, H. (2002) 'Critical Literacy Methods, Models and Motivations'. Presentation given at the National Council of Teachers Annual Convention in Atlanta Georgia.

Kress, G. & van Leeuwen, T. (1996) *Reading Images: The Grammar of Visual Design*. London: RoutledgeFalmer Press.

Luke, A. (1998) 'Getting Over Method: Literacy Teaching as Work in New Times', *Language Arts*, 75 (4), 305–13.

Luke, C. (1997) 'Media literacy and cultural studies', in S. Muspratt, A. Luke & P. Freebody (eds) *Constructing Critical Literacies: Teaching and Learning Textual Practice*. Cresskill, NJ: Hampton Press.

Luke, A., O'Brien, J. & Comber, B. (1994) 'Making Community Texts Objects of Study', *Australian Journal of Language and Literacy*, 17 (2), 139–49.

O'Brien, J. (1998) 'Experts in Smurfland', in M. Knobel & A. Healy (eds) *Critical Literacy in the Primary Classroom*. Newton, New South Wales: Primary English Teaching Association.

Time magazine cover (1999) Vol.153 (18).

Vasquez, V. (2003) 'What Pokemon can teach us about learning and literacy', *Language Arts*, 81 (2), 118–25.

Vasquez, V. (2004a) *Negotiating Critical Literacies with Young Children*. Mahwah, NJ: Lawrence Erlbaum Associates.

Vasquez, V. (2004b) 'Resistance, power-tricky, and colorless energy: what engagement with everyday popular culture texts can teach us about learning and literacy', in J. Marsh (ed.) *Popular Culture, Media and Digital Literacies in Early Childhood*. London: RoutledgeFalmer Press.

Vasquez, V. (in press) 'Doing critical literacy with young children: using the everyday to take up issues of social justice and equity in a pre-school setting', in C. Luna & J. Willet (eds) *Doing Critical Literacy in Hard Times*.

CHAPTER 6

Beanie Babies

An opportunity to promote literacy development or a money-spinner for the business tycoons?

Janet Evans

What do children think about the manufacture and product marketing of popular culture icons? As child consumers, do they feel pressured into buying popular culture artefacts? Are they motivated by working with popular culture icons as a purpose for collaborative writing? These questions and others are considered in this chapter which focuses on work done with ten- and 11-year-old children. It draws on transcriptions of their discussions, recordings of collaborative writing sessions and their responses to a series of questions relating to Beanie Babies, their origins, their intended market audience and their creator's entrepreneurial intentions in relation to the global marketplace. Finally it takes a closer look at children's views of the manufacturers who make, advertise and sell these types of popular toys and explores children's relationship to the consumerist deology, which surrounds popular culture.

Introduction

> Men are like Beeny Babies . . . they're cheap, their heads are mushy, and the really cute ones are hard to find.

These words found in a birthday card (Figure 6.1) show just how much Beanie Babies have entered the psyche of both children and adults because to be able to understand the card one must be aware of Beanie Babies and their marketing qualities.

This chapter considers some of the views of a group of ten- and 11-year-old children in relation to Beanie Babies as popular culture icons but also investigates some of the influences on the marketing of popular culture icons since the beginning of this century and more recently. I initially became interested in Beanie Babies after using them as artefacts to accompany book reading sessions. All of the children, whatever

Men are like Beeny-Babies.

They're cheap, their heads are mushy, and the really cute ones are hard to find.

Figure 6.1 (Original design by Tomato Cards. All rights reserved. Recycled Paper Greetings, Inc. Reprinted by permission.)

their ages, loved the Beanie Babies and wanted to hold them or play with them while the book was being read. They were very motivated to talk about the latest addition to their personal collections of Beanie Babies or about the latest Beanie Babies news. I did not realise the full impact of Beanie Babies as toys, collectors' items, cult icons and representations of the culture industry at work, until we had friends to stay for a few days; their three young daughters had one collective goal in mind, to go shopping for Beanie Babies and to buy the latest ones for their collection. They were hooked and so was I! They on buying Beanie Babies for their growing collection, me on the idea that these children seemed to be, without knowing it, being manipulated to buy, buy, buy, from the big consumer producers. As children (the youngest being just four years old), they had already stepped aboard the ever-expanding, continually moving youth market conveyer belt and were being commercially exploited by the big multinationals. Beanie Babies represent just one miniscule part of this exploitation and being a Beanie Babies collector signified to these children that they were, in certain circles, a member of the 'club' and therefore cool (Klein 2001).

The branding of toys

At the beginning of the twenty-first century, possessions in general and toys in particular play a very important part in the lives of contemporary Western children.

Kline (1993) has documented the development of children as consumers of toys and has looked at the influences on this development through the last century. The reasons for the success of the toy in marketing terms are complex and varied but at the forefront is the manufacturer's ability to 'capture' children through inventive television programmes, through persuasive advertising and marketing, and through film tie-ins. High-profile image branding making use of specialist logos and peer group pressure fuelled the rise in youth culture in a two-way process that fed off the market consumption of products. Corporations realised that children themselves needed to be targeted and many successful companies conducted market research focusing on children. This use of clever and expert market research, based on asking children what they wanted, was a powerful way of tapping into the growing, influential pre-teen and youth culture. It is very evident that children are potent, influential consumers. Kenway and Bullen (2001) in their work looking at children as consumers state that, '. . . consumer-media culture in its various forms has transformed the lives of children, the institutions of the family and the school and, ultimately, the "nature" of childhood' (p. 8).

From the 1930s onwards the 'culture industry' (Adorno 1991) was targeting children specifically as its main audience. In the 1920s and early 1930s Disney was perfecting the fairy-tale film genre through great advances in technological expertise and at this time children were seen as consumers in a double sense: of films and of consumer products linked to the films (DeCordova 1994). Film studios, with Disney in the lead, rapidly spotted the marketing potential of producing film-related products for a willing audience and now there is such a tremendous demand that film-linked videos, cassettes, T-shirts, ties, jewellery, pottery figures, toys, books and other 'tie-in' artefacts are commonplace and are purchased in huge quantities by a demanding, eager, young and not so young audience. In manufacturing these film tie-in products Disney's prime concern was the promotion of himself and of the copyrighted Disney label – all of the products were branded – clearly marked with the famous Disney logo. The Disney drive to capture children as consumers was linked, not to a philanthropic desire to nurture their cultural needs because of the artistic merit of the films, but rather to the intention of exercising total control over children's aesthetic interests and consumer tastes. They wanted to completely capture the market with their goods and to take over the market with the brand name, it was the copyrighted label that mattered most (for further information on this see Zipes 1997). By capitalising on children's desire to become at one with their favourite pop-culture icons, multinational super brands have merged and synergised to ensure that they are part and parcel of every child's (and adults') daily lifestyle (Klein 2001). This merging and synergising is taken one stage further by what Hade and Edmondson (2003), in their work looking at the effect of commercialisation on children's book publishing, call *cross-promoting*. They state that, '. . . each spin-off piece of merchandise, and each retelling across another medium, becomes a promotion for every other product based on that story' and that 'This ubiquitous *cross-promoting* blurs, if not erases, the line between advertising and entertainment' (p.139).

Children and the culture industry

It is clear from these early origins of branded consumer goods that children and young people are key players in the culture industry. Marketing corporations know that they need hooking from as early an age as possible. Denby (1996) feels that children are in an almost impossible situation and notes that, 'By the time they are five or six, they've been pulled into the marketplace. They're on their way to becoming not citizens but consumers' (p. 7).

Zipes (1997) in agreement with this viewpoint states that some advocates of popular culture:

> . . . fail to grasp how early the media penetrate the lives of children, how strong is the referential system of the culture industry, and how it sets the terms for socialization and education in the Western world. Cultural institutions in the twentieth century are centred around profit, power and pleasure through power. It is how we learn about and make use of power strategies that gives us some sense of autonomy and pleasure. Popular culture is a myth because we cannot assume that what emanates from 'the people' is theirs, that is, an expression of their authentic desires or wishes. These desires and wishes are not ours – even when we think they are or would like them to be – because we tend to forget what the culture industry does to our children and ourselves.
>
> (p. 8)

So, what does the culture industry do to our children? Adorno (1991) spoke on behalf of individuality, originality, uniqueness and particularism. He also spoke against the conformity of the masses. He was aware that most people, while belonging to the masses, also thought they were individual and unique beings. Therein lies the dilemma. How can the culture industry manage to make huge numbers of people think they are unique and individual while at the same time compelling them to conform to market forces and subscribe to political organisations whose main function is to expand the capitalist production of commodities? How can people be made to purchase things that they do not really want or need?

Klein (2001), in a wide-ranging investigation into consumer capitalism, branding and the global economy, is under no illusion that the culture industry, controlled by multinationals, has deliberately, in fact systematically, stripped many young people of the opportunity to make choices while at the same time allowing them to think there are many more choices to be made among the diverse range of consumer products which is available:

> The branded multinationals may talk diversity, but the visible result of their actions is an army of teen clones marching – in 'uniform,' as the marketers say – into the global mall. Despite the embrace of polyethnic imagery, market-driven globalization doesn't

want diversity, quite the opposite. Its enemies are national habits, local brands and distinctive regional tastes. Fewer interests control ever more of the landscape.

(p.129)

Klein (2001) documents the rise of the multinationals from the early twentieth century to today with a particular focus on the last 20 years. She notes how the rise of the product brand, the creating of an image, a lifestyle, a way of being, steadily took over from mere advertising. Advertising simply conveys a product's existence to the world, whereas branding is 'the core meaning of the modern corporation' (p. 5). This 'meaning' or 'brand essence' is represented by the corporate logo and moves the consumers' thoughts away from the product onto an image of a desirable lifestyle. Thus the logo conjures up not just a product to be bought but a whole way of life, an attitude, a set of values to be sought. Moving on from branding products, the corporations started to brand the media, music, sports, stars and eventually even educational establishments. Multinational companies such as Nike, Disney, Starbucks, Calvin Klein, Coca Cola, were all branding and expanding and they were doing it to the masses. Worldwide this meant that the masses all got the same message regardless of their culture or ethnic background, everyone was carefully guided into wanting a slice of the same good lifestyle cake; they were becoming homogenised and in the process globalised.

Targeting the youth market

It was the youth market that embraced this branded culture industry with most vigour with the branding of television and music, particular domains of the young, being mostly responsible for this. The multinationals were not slow to realise who the most important market was and they targeted certain areas with even more rigour: food, drink, jeans, music, sportswear, hairstyles, magazines, role models, nothing was left unturned in the drive to capture the audience. Choice was rapidly becoming unattainable; consumers, and in particular young consumers, could only buy, and indeed only wanted to buy, what everyone else had. They were cloned but were made to feel cool at the same time – they were part of the culture club.

Adorno (1991) felt the recipe for success in any Western capitalist society was the surrender of individualism, while Zipes (1997) maintained that:

> In order to maximize profit, the culture industry has to instil standard expectations in audiences so that they think they are getting what they want, and that by getting what they supposedly want, they can become like the stars with whom they identify. When accused of 'dumbing down' their programs and products, corporate representatives in the culture industry are fond of announcing that they are conceding to the wishes of the public and are only as guilty as their audiences. Of course they never mention that they seek to control these audiences through their own polls and conditioning processes. The culture industry is indeed 'totalitarian' – perhaps one should use the

word *global* today, given the globalization of corporate capitalism – in its intention to totally take over markets and dominate demands and wishes.

(p. 7)

As already stated, this domination of demands and wishes starts young. Dyson (1997), Hilton (1996), Kinder (1991), Kline (1993), Marsh and Millard (2000; 2003), and Scott (2000) have all looked at the production, marketing and use of toys and games by young children. In the early 1900s the toy market targeted wealthy, middle-class adults (Kline 1993; Seiter 1995). However, the twentieth century saw a move to marketing directly targeted at children themselves. The appeal to young people to become part of the 'cool' youth culture by wearing the 'right' kind of clothes, listening to the 'right' kind of music, eating the 'right' kind of food, and in general conforming to the kind of mould that the multinationals have provided was nurtured at every opportunity by film tie-ins, toys with meals, non-stop music television (MTV) and other similar consumer-led ideas which prove membership of *the* club.

The branding of Beanie Babies

Ty Warner has branded his merchandise flawlessly. Beanie Babies, although not marketed in the traditional manner through advertising and through sales in major retail outlets, fit the consumer market perfectly. The Ty Warner marketing department, in order to capitalise on the growing youth subculture when marketing Beanie Babies, has managed:

> to create 'special symbols' or situations for the youth market niche, and . . . the use of peer group processes as a means of social involvement and persuasion. Together these approaches combined to create the 'youth ethos' that helped to manage youth as a separate part of the marketplace.
>
> (Hilton 1996: 165)

Scott (2000) in looking at what Beanie Babies teach children notes that Ty Warner has been careful to market these soft beanbag toys in a very select, quite unusual manner which has not included mass marketing and advertising. In America they are sold in local, low-profile outlets as opposed to huge superstores and it is the creation and cultivation of a Beanie Babies network for children that has really done the selling. Children, who are usually members of the Beanie Babies Official Club, pass on information about where to find the latest Beanie Babies by word of mouth, they search the Internet and they network with other Beanie Babies collectors. Ty Warner has made young people feel cool and sophisticated. As Scott states:

> Undermarketing induces a high level of commitment by kids to the Beanie market, since their knowledge of Beanies allows them to feel invested in, and dependent on, everything that Beanies represent. Beanies grant kids a level of autonomy and freedom

that is both appealing and powerful, allow them to define themselves in unique ways that defy adult notions of childhood innocence, and encourage them to take bolder steps into the magical world of marketing and consumption.

(p. 8)

Scott points out that Beanie Babies are more than suitable for 'cultural invasion and colonization of young minds in the globalization of markets' (p. 9). In buying and collecting Beanie Babies, children as consumers are creating new worlds, new identities and therefore new cultures that separate them from the world of adults. They revel in the freedom to both create and be created by the products they choose to have in their lives and this in itself gives them a feeling of real power despite the fact that they are being manipulated as consumers to buy what is on offer.

Popular culture characters as a stimulus: working with the children

A personal interest in using popular culture artefacts to promote literacy activities led me to use Beanie Babies as a stimulus for collaborative shared and guided writing with ten- and 11-year-old children. Alongside the literacy activities my aim was to conduct a general investigation into the children's thoughts about Beanie Babies to include:

- who they thought produced them and why;
- what the children thought about their roles as consumers in the Beanie Babies market;
- whether they felt they were being manipulated in the global marketing campaign;
- whether they felt the buying, playing with and collecting of Beanie Babies was a gendered activity.

I worked intensively with a group of five children, three girls and two boys, for six half-day periods. The class teacher chose children who were willing to talk freely and share their ideas. They proved to be confident, articulate youngsters who were not afraid of expressing a point of view.

At the start of our first session I took five Beanie Babies into class and asked the children to jot down what they thought about them. Then we shared thoughts and ideas. Although I had initiated this opening discussion, the agenda was soon appropriated by the children whose ideas came fast and furious once they were stimulated by the subject matter. Each of the six sessions became part of a continuum, each starting where the previous one had finished. All sessions were tape-recorded and the children's work saved. We worked on nine different activities. After the first four activities (below), the others were all initiated by the children alone. They included:

1   A questionnaire filled in by 117 children.

2   A brief written overview of what they thought about Beanie Babies prior to any discussion/activities.

3   In-depth discussion stimulated by a variety of Beanie Babies which were taken to session along with a *Mary Beth's Bean Bag World Monthly* magazine and other Beanie Babies memorabilia.

4   Inventing a new Beanie Babie and writing biographical details to describe it.

5   Reading 'Ty tag' poems from existing Beanie Babies and making up new poems for the Beanie Babies they had invented.

6   Planning for and organising points of view to hold a debate for and against the business ethics of Ty Warner, the entrepreneur and creator of Beanie Babies.

7   Designing a Ty Warner, 'Wanted for Deceit' poster.

8   Creating a capitalist 'rogues' gallery' to include names, description of organisations, origins, accusations against them, winners and losers of the capitalist system.

9   A further written overview of what they thought about Beanie Babies after all the intensive discussions and activities had taken place. Comparisons were made with the initial overviews.

Out of the nine activities it was the group discussion, the work on the capitalist 'rogues' gallery', the 'Wanted for Deceit' posters, and the comparisons between the *before* and *after* statements that were most illuminating in relation to how they viewed themselves as consumers in a capitalist society.

Group discussion

Initially the children had been asked to jot down their views of Beanie Babies. The views were short and simple indicating that they thought Beanie Babies were just cute, cuddly toys and nothing more. These written comments led onto an in-depth discussion and their thoughts, stimulated by the collaborative group discussion, were incredibly complex and wide-ranging, showing a critical awareness of how the marketing of Beanie Babies could affect individuals and lifestyles. Their conversation continually linked Beanie Babies to money and capital gains and it led me to ask what Ty Warner, the creator of these soft toys, was doing. The children (names changed) clearly listened to and thought about each other's viewpoints which were insightful and perceptive. This discussion was intense, fast and extremely focused:

John: He's conning us – making us buy Beanie Babies.

Jess: Yes, but he's not conning us, he doesn't advertise Beanie Babies – he never said they are collectables but people decide they are – adults organise Beanie Babies parties. Adults buy Beanie Babies as presents when they are away (working away from home). Adults buy, not children. Rich people buy; they're not aimed at children.

Sophie: Younger people buy – under eight years.

Caroline: No, I don't agree, they're aimed at over 11 years and adults because they are collecting.

John: Going back to Jessica's point of working mums travelling and buying Beanie Babies because they feel guilty about being away from home – it's a guilt trip.

David: They should sell them cheaper to get more money.

Jess: No, they need to be more expensive.

Me: But Ty Warner sells at a price and it is the collectors who set the going rate.

Caroline: Disney babies sell for even more.

John: Other companies are cashing in on his idea because they see him getting more money. I think they should make them cheaper – three at £10 each are the same as six at £5 each.

Me: Did Ty Warner intend other companies to get into the production of Beanie Babies?

Caroline: It would be good to interview Ty Warner.

Sophie: I think he did intend us to get worked up because then there would be a greater interest in the Babies.

John: I don't think he did. He intended to make people happy at first, initially he did it as a hobby, this took off, then he used a factory . . .

David: (*interrupting*) . . . I can't see that – he wanted to make lots of money from the beginning. He got the idea – it will make lots of money – he shows it to a toy factory and they make loads of money for him.

Jess: Although there was no advertising, they got people interested in 'rare' versions.

Sophie: Quite clever really, isn't it?

David: He's scaring people into buying them – they want every one of them so he (Ty Warner) 'retires' them and this makes certain ones more desirable.

Sophie: I think he wanted to be rich from the beginning . . . he *intended* to be rich from the beginning.

David: It's the name that does it . . . like Bill Gates with Microsoft. People buy him because of the name, it's well respected . . . They buy because they know it is good.

John: Bill Gates made so much money that other companies took him to court.

David: Apple Mac is good!

Me: Are there any similarities between Ty Warner and Bill Gates? They both seem to make a lot of money.

John: The difference between the two is that Bill Gates has made something useful as opposed to a bit of fur stuffed with beans. Computers are the mainstay of the USA and the world. To give him his credit, he was very clever . . . (*pause – next bit said with a twinkle in his eyes*) . . . I think we'd better stop this conversation or else we'll be going to the anti-capitalist riots in Seattle.

David: We need computers but do we need Beanie Babies?

John: Bill Gates and Ty Warner started off with the same kind of idea but they branched off. Both of them are manipulating people, more so with Ty Warner, for example if you rob someone you go to prison but if you sell Beanie Babies you don't.

Me: Who's making the decision to buy?

David: Friends are making the decision – they can make you buy. Friends are making you buy. It's the same with mobile phones.

John: They (the Ty Warner and Bill Gates companies) are making us make the decision.

Me: Are we being manipulated?

Jess: Yes and no – half and half.

Sophie: At the end of the day it's your decision whether to buy or not.

John: Friends *are* manipulating you to buy.

Sophie: I don't think it is friends, for example with mobile phones, I don't want one and *all* my friends ask why I haven't got one.

At this point the conversation had to stop as it was lunchtime. At the start of the discussion the girls, who were more pro-Beanie Babies than the boys, had been defensive of the product and of Ty Warner, while the boys, initially more anti-Beanie Babies, were critical of the product and of its effect on society. These polarised views did, however, become more centralised as they listened to and shared each other's viewpoints. The discussion had considered:

- Beanie Babies as collectors' items which make money;
- Limited edition Beanie Babies which sell for higher prices;
- Ways in which shops make it difficult to buy newly released, highly priced Beanie Babies;
- The way in which shops make commission through the number of Beanie Babies they sell;
- How the myriad types of Beanie Babies encourage collectors to keep on buying;
- The comparison between playing football and collecting Beanie Babies, the former being a collaborative game with winners and losers, the latter being a collector's 'game' whereby the only winners are the sellers, that is, the shops that sell Beanie Babies and Ty Warner.

The rogues' gallery of business tycoons

The children had been keen, animated and highly motivated by the above, fast-moving discussion. They had made several suggestions for the topic of our next session but it was the rogues' gallery with all the big business tycoons – Bill Gates, Ty Warner, Walt Disney, Nike, Reebok and McDonalds – that they chose to focus on (Figure 6.2).

The children's responses showed how aware they were of the place of Beanie Babies in the toy marketplace. Their responses also showed how Ty Warner, the producer of Ty Inc. and Beanie Babies, ranked in the global marketplace in relation to other big business conglomerates. Comments were scribed on a large grid as the conversation ranged from how children were part of a carefully planned campaign to get them to buy Beanie Babies and then become Beanie Babies collectors (by retiring them and bringing out limited editions), to whether Ty Warner and entrepreneurs like him are immoral and should be charged with using cheap labour? Their perceptive discussions considered if children, and seemingly their parents, were being exposed to a huge great entrepreneurial marketing ploy. Kenway and Bullen (2001), in considering some of the historical trends in relation to consumer children, note that:

> Without doubt, the consuming child of the West is the beneficiary of labouring children of such countries as Indonesia, China and Pakistan. The 'dark side' of such celebrated brands names as Nike, Disney and Mattel involves impoverished and highly exploitative sweatshop production conditions for young people in these countries.
>
> (p. 37)

The children were clearly making links between the production of Beanie Babies and other mass-marketed goods by the multinationals that seem to be steadily homogenising the world through sales of their branded products and lifestyles. Beanie Babies can be seen as a metaphor for post-modern life, in which we are bombarded with false worlds; the 'unique, genuine' world we create for ourselves may be nothing more than a bricolage of all the false worlds we have been exposed to.

Designing 'Wanted for Deceit' posters

The children decided that something should be done about Ty Warner as a 'rip-off merchant'. They said they thought he was a deceitful character and in looking up the meaning of the word 'deceit' in the dictionary, they found it was like saying one thing and doing another. They decided to design 'Wanted for Deceit' posters and prior to starting, they brainstormed their ideas and drafted them in rough (see Figure 6.3).

They carefully considered what essential features of language would be needed to attract readers to this kind of poster and came up with: bold headlines; graphics that grab the reader's attention; use of strong colours; and a simple but informative

Gallery of Business Tycoons (conmen, rogues and fraudsters)

	Ty Warner	Bill Gates	Walt Disney	Warner Bros.	McDonalds	Nike	Reebok	Manchester United
Organisation	Makes Beanie Babies – soft toys.	• Computer production & software. • Inventor of Microsoft. • World's richest man.	• Makes films, books, soft toys, theme parks. • Directs films. • Invented & wrote stories. • Established merchandiser shops.	• Films, books, soft toys, theme parks, merchandiser shops. (Same as for Walt Disney)	• Fast food company. • World's most successful food corporation (money-wise).	• Sports clothing & equipment. • Shops	(Same as for Nike)	• Football team • Shops and merchandise. • Football shirts. • TV channel. • Promoting – buying & selling footballers.
Origin	USA	USA	USA	USA	USA	USA	UK	UK
Accusation	Using the 'Ahh' factor to make money.	• Overpowering small companies. • Not giving anyone else a chance at conquering market. • Stopping freedom of choice.	• Using his characters & logo to sell almost anything and make money. • Using other people's ideas for his gain (£).	(See Disney)	• Destroying rainforests for material gains (capitalism). • Discouraging healthy living. • Too many additives (salt). • Sacrificing quality for gain, watering down drinks, selling cheap, nasty rubbish. • Pressurising us to buy 'cause they're swamping us with stores.	• Charging too much. • Using child and cheap labour. • Charging for the logo. • Chasing the popular market for children & adults, e.g. PlayStation. • Making games with Nike label to attract children.	(See Nike)	• Bringing out 20 kits in ten seasons – swamping the market. • Appealing to children 'cause they are the ones who want the new kit. • Changing styles quickly to sell goods. • Putting logo on everything to sell goods. • Overpaying players – money could go into things that could help society.
Winners	The corporations themselves!							
Losers	The consumers and the whole world!							

Figure 6.2 Typed version of the children's rogues' gallery of business tycoons

supporting text. Working collaboratively in groups, they produced two posters, both of which were very effective in relation to their audience and purpose (see Figure 6.4).

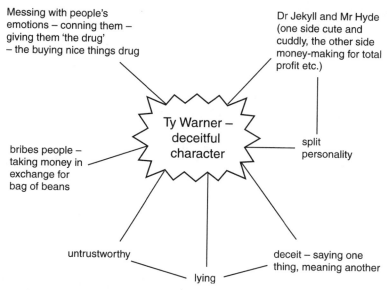

Messing with people's emotions – conning them – giving them 'the drug' – the buying nice things drug

Dr Jekyll and Mr Hyde (one side cute and cuddly, the other side money-making for total profit etc.)

Ty Warner – deceitful character

bribes people – taking money in exchange for bag of beans

split personality

untrustworthy

lying

deceit – saying one thing, meaning another

Figure 6.3 Brainstorm for Ty Warner 'Wanted for Deceit' poster

In drawing an analogy between what they considered to be Ty Warner's deceitful activities and those of an infamous criminal, John stated, 'It is like a case of Dr Jekyll and Mr Hyde: cute, cuddly teddies on one side, money-making profits and all that on the other.' He went on to say. 'He [Ty Warner] is luring you in and giving you "the drug". Once you've bought one or two [Beanies], it's difficult to stop. You have to carry on.' These children were becoming really involved with the issues. Caroline said, 'He's messing with people's emotions on one side by making them [Beanie Babies] cute then charging a lot of money.'

Before and after statements compared

The short period of time spent working with these five children was amazing. The initial discussion about popular culture characters quickly led to other things that interested them and eventually on to complex, philosophical debates on the economic and social structures of society. The in-depth discussions looking at popular culture from a critical, socially perceptive standpoint (Gee 1993) indicated that these children, far from being unaware that they were manipulated, were incredibly conscious of exactly how they were being positioned in today's marketplace. They knew they were being influenced by the huge multinational consortiums and by Ty Warner with his sales of Beanie Babies. The children's before and after statements clearly demonstrated their growing sophistication in relation to themselves as consumers and yet despite this awareness their comments still indicated that they would continue to buy (girls) and not buy (boys).

Jessica

Before

Beanie Babies are really cute and can be worth quite a lot of money. They are nice things to keep from your childhood.

After

Beanie Babies are cute and I am still going to buy them, but now that I have realised that the person manufacturing them is a 'rip-off merchant' I will not buy as many. These few days [discussing] have made me think that the manufacturers aren't making them for our enjoyment; they're making them for money. The people making them are the winners. We are not.

Caroline

Before

I think that Beanies are soft animal toys that are collectors' items.

After

I still think that Beanies are really cute and I am still going to carry on buying them although I am now aware that Ty Warner is a business tycoon and rips you off. I now understand that he is the winner and we are the losers.

Sophie

Before

I think Beanie Babies are really cute and some are very valuable and are collectors' items.

After

I think that Beanies are really cute and I'm going to continue buying them. After the discussions and debates we have had I am more aware of the facts and how Ty Warner is ripping us off.

David

Before

I think that they are interesting but I wouldn't want to collect them because they're just a stuffed toy.

After

I think that Beanies are OK but I still wouldn't want to buy them because they're just a big money-making scam so the producer (Ty Warner) gets lots of money. I think it made me realise what was happening by discussing.

John

Before

I think that Beanies are overrated and that there are many better ways to use money.

After

I think that, to many people, Beanies can be quite interesting but I still see them as a useless thing to spend money on. The discussions have made me realise the cute side of Beanies but not enough to change my views.

Figure 6.4 One of the 'Wanted for Deceit' posters

Conclusions

Children are now seen as consumers in their own right (McNeil 1992; Kenway & Bullen 2001; Lee 1993, 2000). They are seen as a marketing sector that needs nurturing because they have substantial amounts of money of their own to spend; they are able to influence the way money is spent in their home environments; and they are society's future adult consumers. The Beanie Babies activities enabled the children to reflect on the decisions they made in everyday life; decisions in relation to making choices about what they buy, eat, drink, listen to etc. The children's critical discussion, focusing on the money-making tactics and marketing techniques used by Ty Warner and other consumer capitalists, was easily translated into an overall awareness of how the actions of big multinationals affect us.

The project started in an open-ended manner; I was hoping to create opportunities for critical conversations in relation to Beanie Babies as popular culture characters and their place in the present marketplace, along with consideration of some literacy-based activities using Beanie Babies as a stimulus to collaborative writing. It finished up as an investigation into consumer capitalism aimed at the ever-expanding youth culture. After six intensive half-days I was left with many unanswered questions related to children's detailed knowledge about consumer capitalism and themselves as consumers.

In this ever-changing age of consumerism we need to provide children with opportunities to reflect critically, in discerning ways, on the lives they are living. This ability is already there in some children but needs nurturing and extending to all. The combination of literacy-based activities, discussion and the opportunity for self-reflection certainly proved to be a successful method for enabling these children to think critically. Using popular culture artefacts in the classroom situation can provide many different starting points for reflective thought and therefore closer investigation into the way we are positioned to lead our lives in a dynamic, capitalist society where events and happenings are not always as innocuous as they are often portrayed.

Implications for practice

- **Provide children with opportunities to respond to important issues**

This means being aware of what children are interested in; providing non-threatening situations in which to talk; keeping an open mind; respecting all responses; and organising the classroom for small group discussions to take place.

- **Encourage children to be critical consumers in today's marketplace**

Encourage children to question popular culture texts and artefacts in relation to:

- Who created the message and why?

–   What techniques are being used to attract my attention?

–   Who is the message aimed at; who is missed out of this message?

–   What views and lifestyles are represented?

–   How might people from different backgrounds and cultures interpret this message?

(Adapted from Thoman 1999)

● **Use children's popular culture interests as starting points for literacy activities**

With specific reference to Beanie Babies consider:

–   Inventing new Beanie Babies and writing biographical details to describe them.

–   Reading 'Ty tag' poems from existing Beanie Babies and making up new poems for the newly invented Beanie Babies.

–   Planning for and organising a debate for and against the business practices of Ty Warner, the creator of Beanie Babies.

References

Adorno, T. (1991) *The Culture Industry*. London: Routledge.

DeCordova, R. (1994) 'The Mickey in Macy's Window: Childhood, Consumerism and Disney Animation', in E. L. Smoodin (ed.) (1994) *Disney Discourse: Producing the Magic Kingdom*. New York: Routledge.

Denby, D. (1996) 'Buried Alive: Our Children and the Avalanche of Crud', *The New Yorker*, 72, 15 July 1996: 52.

Dyson, A.H. (1997) *Writing Superheroes: Contemporary Childhood, Popular Culture and Classroom Literacy*. New York: Teachers College Press.

Gee, J. (1993) 'Critical Literacy/Socially Perceptive Literacy: A Study of Language in Action', in H. Fehring & P. Green (eds) *Critical Literacy: A Collection of Articles from the Australian Literacy Educators' Association*. Delaware: International Reading Association.

Hade, D. & Edmondson, J. (2003) 'Children's Book Publishing in Neoliberal Times', in *Language Arts*, 81 (2), 135–43.

Hilton, M. (ed.) (1996) *Potent Fictions: Children's Literacy and the Challenge of Popular Culture*. London: Routledge.

Kenway, J. & Bullen, E. (2001) *Consuming Children: Education – Entertainment-Advertising*. Buckingham: Open University Press.

Kinder, M. (1991) *Playing with Power in Movies: Television and Video Games from Muppet Babies to Teenage Mutant Ninja Turtles*. Berkeley, CA: University of California Press.

Klein, N. (2001) *No Logo*. London: Flamingo.

Kline, S. (1993) *Out of the Garden: Toys and Children's Culture in the Age of TV Marketing*. London: Verso.

Lee, M.J. (1993) *Consumer Culture Reborn: The Cultural Politics of Consumption*. London: Routledge.

Lee, M.J. (ed.) (2000) *The Consumer Society Reader*. Malden: Blackwell.

Marsh, E. & Millard, E. (2000) *Literacy and Popular Culture: Using Children's Culture in the Classroom*. London: Paul Chapman.

Marsh, E. & Millard, E. (2003) *Literacy and Popular Culture in the Classroom*. Reading: National Centre for Language and Literacy, The University of Reading.

McNeil, J.U. (1992) *Kids as Customers: A Handbook of Marketing to Children*. New York: Lexington Books.

Scott, D. (2000) 'What Are Beanie Babies Teaching Our Children?' in G. Canella & J. Kincheloe (eds) *Kidsworld*. New York: Peter Lang.

Seiter, E. (1995) *Sold Separately: Children and Parents in Consumer Culture*. New Brunswick: Rutgers University Press.

Thoman, E. (1999) 'Media Literacy! Skills and strategies for media education', *Education Leadership*, 56 (5), 50–54.

Zipes, J. (1997) *Happily Ever After: Fairy Tales, Children and the Culture Industry*. London: Routledge.

CHAPTER 7

Children reread and rewrite their local neighbourhoods: critical literacies and identity work

Barbara Comber and Helen Nixon

This chapter considers the complex literate repertoires of twenty-first century children in multicultural primary classrooms in Adelaide South Australia. It draws on the curricular and pedagogical work of two experienced primary school teachers who explore culture, race and class, by positioning children as textual producers across a variety of media. In particular we discuss two child-authored texts: *A is for Arndale*, a local alphabet book co-authored by children aged between eight and ten, and *Cooking Afghani Style*, a magazine-style film produced by a mixed-aged class of children (aged eight to 13) recently arrived in Australia. In the process of making these texts, primary children engaged in reading as a cultural practice, rereading and rewriting texts related to their neighbourhoods and to their identities (both individual and collective). This involved frequent excursions to local key sites, both familiar and unfamiliar to the children. They investigated how diverse children experienced and lived their lives in particular places within changing communities.

Introduction

Critical literacy, as a concept, has a long history, most notably from Paolo Freire's (1970) political work with poor communities in South America. However, in terms of primary school literacy curriculum and policy its emergence is relatively recent. Critical literacy involves teachers exploring with children how texts work to have particular effects in particular situations. Teachers who take a critical approach to literacy understand that language and images involve power relations; that writers, producers, advertisers and everyday conversationalists use particular words and images and not others. Their products – texts – can exclude and include and position listeners, readers and viewers in different ways. When teachers assist children to become critically literate, they encourage them to question taken-for-granted aspects of storybook worlds, 'the news', so-called 'factual texts' and so on, and to be aware of the effects that their own decisions as producers of texts might have on their readers, listeners or viewers. A critical approach might direct children's attention to authors' and illustrators' decisions about representation, advertisers' claims, and contested versions of a contemporary or historical event. In other words, a critical literacy approach invites children not only to crack the code, make meaning and use texts, but also to analyse texts (following Luke & Freebody 1999) – considering both how they work and what work they do in the world. A further aim, on which we focus here, is to reposition children as 'active designers and agents' in shaping social futures (Luke 2000: 449).

In Australia, educators have been working on critical approaches to literacy education for almost two decades. Such approaches have not been reserved for high school or university English classes, but also explored with young children (O'Brien 1994; Luke, Comber & O'Brien 1996). From the start of school, children have been introduced to text-analytic approaches whereby they might consider the grammars and vocabularies of toy catalogues, food packaging and other everyday texts, the roles of mothers and fathers, boys and girls in children's literature, and the kinds of 'science facts' that publishers believe are appropriate for young readers (O'Brien 2001). In other words, young children have learnt to 'problematise' and deconstruct texts, not only to read, use and appreciate.

Much of this text-based analytical work is based on critical discourse analysis (Fairclough 1992; Janks 1993; Luke 1996) and feminist post-structuralist critique (Baker & Davies 1993; Gilbert 1991; O'Brien 2001; Mellor, Patterson & O'Neill 1987). Such approaches have children look at the ways language and images work to represent and misrepresent, include and exclude, and maintain dominant discourses. (Dominant discourses are those that present the views of the most powerful and influential in society at a particular time.) The work of anti-racist and feminist educators also had an impact. We do not review this history of critical literacy's emergence in Australia here (see Comber 1994, 2003; Luke 2000). We simply note that earlier developments focused mainly on text analysis. More recent developments in critical literacy focus not only on what children read and view, but also on what they design, compose and produce across a range of genres, media and modes (Janks 2000, 2003; Kamler 2001; New London Group 1996; Searle 1993).

In this chapter we turn our attention also to the ways critical literacy pedagogies, broadly conceived, might assist young people to assemble productive social practices and discursive resources (by which we mean those ways of operating that young people need to fully participate in representative democracies – for example, negotiation, respect for difference and familiarity with powerful genres). As will become clear, text analysis and questions about language, culture and power are embedded in these pedagogies, but the interrogation of texts in this curriculum is less visible than is the production of texts. We understand these as 'counter-narratives' because they disrupt the relations around school textual practices – reading, writing and viewing – that usually hold. We discuss how two teachers working in highly multicultural and socio-economically diverse schools reposition primary-aged children as ethnographers of everyday life and contemporary multimedia chroniclers and commentators. In two separate school locations, Marg Wells and Helen Grant work with their children to enlist the resources of the neighbourhood, to produce and publish texts about their ways of life: *A is for Arndale*, an alphabet book, and *Cooking Afghani Style*, a short film.

If as literacy educators we want children to learn that texts matter – typically a key goal of literacy teaching in general – then children need to be involved in producing texts that matter to them; they need to experience the serious investment required to produce school texts that go beyond the school desk, the teacher's bag, the fridge door or the bin; and they need to experience the level of commitment required to produce artefacts which are aesthetically pleasing and rich with meaning. Studying children's work can illuminate what is being made to count in classrooms and indeed what constitutes normative literate practices. In the cases of these teachers, this work involved children rereading and rewriting texts related to their neighbourhoods and revisiting their complex cultural histories. Such curriculum work is an instance of critical pedagogy and place-based education being brought together – where teachers and children move between study of textual practices and study of the material world – in a highly productive fashion (Gruenewald 2003). Place-based education incorporates a focus on particular localities – for example, the shopping centre, the local park, the cemetery, the river, the market – into the school curriculum as the objects of study.

We begin by outlining key principles applied across a number of instances of critical literacy in primary school classrooms (Comber 2001), based on our collaborative studies with teachers. We then summarise our focal texts, *A is for Arndale* and *Cooking Afghani Style*, the contexts of their production in these classrooms, and we explain how these teachers approached critical literacy through artefact production and what was accomplished through this work. We conclude with some suggestions for practice and questions for further classroom inquiry.

Principles informing critical literacy practices

Educators who have worked with critical literacy approaches in their classrooms have been quick to point out that it is not possible to work with any simple formula for critical literacy (see Comber & Simpson 2001; Luke 2000). There is no one way to 'do' critical literacy. This is not to say that anything goes. Rather, each version of critical literacy practice is informed by a number of overarching principles centered around explorations of the connections between language and discourse and unequal power relations. One principle of critical literacy practice is that it 'must address the specificities of the experiences, problems, languages, and histories' of particular communities (McLaren & Giroux 1990: 163). In effect, this means that critical literacy pedagogy will look different for different groups of children in different locations. The local and specific nature of children's lives will always influence what teachers of critical literacy believe is needed and is possible. However, it is precisely from 'the local action with/in particular communities that we can draw some common lessons and principles for re-imagining practice' (Comber 2001: 274).

Reflecting on the common lessons and principles that can be learnt from accounts of how teachers negotiate critical literacies in classrooms across all grade levels (Comber & Simpson 2001), Barbara Comber (2001) notes that teachers' pedagogical moves illustrate a number of 'core dynamic principles and repertoires of practices' which include:

- engaging with local realities;
- researching and analysing language-power relationships, practices and effects;
- mobilising children's knowledges and practices;
- (re)designing texts with political and social intent and real-world use;
- subverting taken-for-granted 'school' texts;
- focusing on children's use of local cultural texts;
- examining how power is exercised and by whom.

(Comber 2001: 276)

The examples described below provide instances of critical literacy curriculum which has been informed by these principles. In addition, these teachers' curriculum has a particular focus on the neighbourhoods surrounding two different schools. Like all critical literacy curriculum, it was designed by teachers who had their particular children's situations and needs in mind. Each teacher's curriculum and pedagogy is critical in that it begins from children's everyday lives, takes their interests into account, and explicitly positions children as researchers and ethnographers of their everyday lives. It is critical pedagogy in action because teachers taught in a way that positioned their children to have agency with respect to researching and documenting topics that matter to them and their communities. In addition, the texts that children produced were designed to include perspectives not often found in 'dominant' cultural texts, and especially not in texts produced by children in schools. Finally, in each case the texts were produced with particular audiences in mind and children knew that their texts would be read and viewed by people beyond the school community.

Film-making as critical literacy practice: *Cooking Afghani Style*

Helen Grant has been teaching in state primary schools for 26 years, mostly as an English as Second Language (ESL) teacher. Grant's work is based on understandings drawn from her reading in the areas of Halliday's (1978) systemic functional linguistics, media studies and critical literacy. In her current role as an ESL teacher in an inner-urban school, Grant takes classes aged from five to 13 years. She works in mainstream classrooms as well as withdrawing groups of ESL children for intensive language work. The school has a strong New Arrivals Program (NAP) for children who have recently arrived in Australia and whose home languages include Arabic, Chinese, Indonesian, Iranian, Kenyan, Khmer, Russian, Serbian and Thai. Grant teaches NAP classes for several lessons a week while their class teachers have 'non-contact time'.

Film-making is a priority for Grant and she has now built an extended body of work with children in this and her previous school. The film *Cooking Afghani Style* was produced with a group of new-arrival ESL children aged 9–12 years. A key goal for literacy teachers working in similar contexts is to encourage children to use their new language – English – to inquire into and talk about their everyday worlds. By talking about the activities and routines of daily life, children learn to communicate with others and gain confidence in using the functional English that they urgently need to learn. Grant shares this ESL goal but she also has an explicit critical literacy agenda, which she pursues by positioning children as researchers of language and culture and as active agents in the production of texts designed for public consumption. Her curriculum is based on the assumption that all children can and should express serious ideas, engage in cultural analysis and produce significant multimedia artefacts (see Luke, Comber & Grant 2003; Nixon & Comber 2004).

Grant's co-productions with children use cultural diversity as both a resource for and the subject of their learning. The children not only include their home languages in the texts they produce, they are also encouraged to make their languages and cultures the subject of inquiry and study. In 2001 and 2002 many Afghani refugees arrived in Grant's 'new arrivals' classes. *Cooking Afghani Style* is a text produced by one of these groups of children Grant taught for several lessons a week over a period of one school term or ten weeks.

What kind of text is *Cooking Afghani Style*? Put simply, it both imitates and subverts the popular lifestyle 'cooking show' genre of television programme popularised in Australia by such chefs as Britain's Jamie Oliver and Nigella Lawson. One thread of the film shows a small group of mixed-age Afghani new-arrival children making popular Afghani dishes. Individuals, pairs and trios are shown talking to camera as they prepare and measure ingredients, assemble and cook the dishes, and share the results with other class and school community members. A second thread of the film shows the children walking through the school's local area – the inner city of Adelaide – a place in which early nineteenth-century South Australian Afghani settlers lived. Children are shown discussing the diverse cultures represented in a restaurant and food market area of the city. We also see them using Arabic, other Afghani languages and English to chat excitedly about landmarks and symbols that indicate the early presence of Afghani people in this area. We see them visit the site of a former camel trader's dwelling, discover a building decorated with the sculpted symbol of a healer and find out that the local Islamic mosque is the oldest in Australia.

Cooking Afghani Style is more than just a cooking show, and this was an integral part of the text's design. As a critical literacy practitioner, it is always Grant's intention to allow children to draw on and represent in multimedia texts their existing knowledges and everyday social practices, whether this be popular culture or Afghani cuisine. In this film children make dishes they have seen made or have made themselves at home. Nonetheless, the planning and production of the texts like this – even where they use children's existing knowledge as a resource – do not happen without a good deal of 'groundwork' on the part of the teacher and the children. In this case, teacher and children together had to research not only the generic features of cooking programmes and recipes for Afghani dishes, but also the history of Afghani people in the inner Adelaide area and in Australian settlement more generally. However, unlike the kinds of 'research' often undertaken by children in school, this research resulted from children's questions about and interest in their daily lives, including their 'place' in their new city, school and country. Further, while some of the research was under-taken using print sources, much of it was literally done 'on the ground'. Children walked the inner-city neighbourhood of the school to learn about its contemporary character as well as its history as an area occupied by Afghani traders over 150 years ago. They also talked with local residents and Afghani community members about cooking and their social histories and occasionally borrowed photographs and printed records, some of which were later incorporated into the film.

The production of *Cooking Afghani Style* therefore involved children 'reading' their local worlds in different ways. It also involved 'writing' the world differently in a text which would, in turn, be read by others. Texts produced in Grant's classes are destined to enter the lives of the classroom and the wider school community and become dynamic texts that continue to have effects long after a curriculum 'unit of work' has been completed. As we have already noted, the rewriting and redesign of texts, to produce countertexts, is a feature of critical literacy practice in that it involves children in contesting dominant ways of viewing the world, which typically marginalise them. In this case, children were positioned to (re)design and produce a text with a political and social intent and real-world use. As a counter-text, *Cooking Afghani Style* contests and complicates dominant representations of children, contemporary 'lifestyles', schooling, and Australian and Afghani history and culture.

The film *Cooking Afghani Style* illustrates the principle of 'redesign' in at least two senses. As we have seen, it works at one level as an alternate version of a lifestyle cooking show. Children are shown introducing and preparing various Afghani dishes and then sharing the finished products with others. The film pro-vides a marked contrast to popular lifestyle cooking shows by having children rather than adults as the presenters, and by featuring simple, everyday dishes produced in their own homes rather than 'exoticising' Afghani fare and the culture. At a more complex level, the film redesigns the lifestyle genre by incorporating aspects of Afghani history and culture, which have remained silenced or hidden within dominant stories of local and national history. Still images of the lives of early Afghani settlers and community leaders are incorporated throughout the film and counterpointed with images of traces of their heritage still visible to contemporary Afghani children who are shown walking the neighbourhood, investigating the street names and symbols and inscriptions to be found there.

Cooking Afghani Style is a powerful example of rewriting or redesign because it is an explicitly political text which was designed to redress the absence of appropriate and up-to-date material about Afghani culture and history available to both Afghani refugee children and other people in the Australian community. We describe these children's work as *re*-design, *re*-write and *re*-imagine to emphasise that such tasks give children the opportunity to *re*-vise, to *re*-work and to change the way things usually are. They are positioned as editors, film-makers, and authors producing new representations of everyday life from their perspectives. The pedagogical practice that produced the text counts as critical literacy practice because it alerted the children to the constructed nature of all texts and to the interested and partial nature of all historical accounts – including their own. From the beginning the teacher made explicit to the children that this film would foreground lesser known facts and stories about Afghani people in Australia. The pedagogical as well as social and political intent was to position the children as agents in helping to counter dominant media stories that demonise refugees. The aim is that children learn – by actually doing it – that they are capable of inserting themselves and their cultural heritage back into living public documents that will make alternative stories of Afghani people available to other children and families.

Reimagining the alphabet book: *A is for Arndale*

Marg Wells has taught young children for over 20 years. For the past seven years she has worked in a poor, highly multicultural, western suburb of Adelaide in two different school communities. She has been involved in a number of school-based projects which emphasise social justice and critical literacy. She has also undertaken classroom research in the use of popular culture in the literacy curriculum. Ridley Grove Primary School, where Wells currently teaches, is located amid a large area designated for 'urban renewal' and housing development during a decade-long change process, which involves the demolition and rebuilding of dwellings on specified streets and the enhancement of local facilities, such as parks and pavements. Like many such sites internationally, the area is a mix of old and new, abandoned, damaged and graffitied structures and spaces, boarded-up windows (see Thomson 2002 for a description of similar areas and the impact on the work of educators). The eight- to ten-year-old children in Wells' class come from many different cultural groups, including Aboriginal, Khmer, Vietnamese, Chinese, Serbian, Philippine, Italian and Anglo-Australian. School policies emphasise developing high-level citizenship and critical literacies in children. Hence Wells is part of a school ethos which is overtly optimistic and ambitious for its children. Wells, in particular, has developed close connections with the developers and personnel associated with the urban renewal project and increasingly 'the neighbourhood' – its changes, future and current conditions form a central part of her curriculum. The current South Australian Curriculum, Standards and Accountability Framework (Department of Education, Training and Employment 2001) includes five 'Essential Learnings': identity, futures, thinking, communication, interdependence. These five areas of the authorised curriculum support Wells' particular approach to critical literacy.

During 2001 and 2002 Wells, the school principal Frank Cairns, and Wells' class were involved in a small research project entitled 'Critical literacy, social action and children's representations of place' along with Pat Thomson and Barbara Comber from the University of South Australia and Hilary Janks from the University of the Witswaterand in Johannesburg, South Africa. We were interested in exploring how children growing up in different places understand their material and social 'place' in the world and in how a critical literacy approach might be productive for teachers and children working in schools in poverty in very different countries. It is part of a move towards critical literacy as reconstructive as well as deconstructive (Janks 2003: 184–5) in the sense that children would be producing as well as analysing texts. It is 'reconstructive' in the sense that children are not simply writing about what is, but also imagining what might be and learning about how other people are living their lives elsewhere. Following from Wells' earlier work on the neighbourhood (Comber, Thomson & Wells 2001) and work being done by Paulina Sethole in constructing vegetable gardens and a curriculum based around the one at her school in Pretoria (Janks 2003), we began to link, in small ways, the principals, teachers and children from the two school communities in South Africa and South Australia. One aspect of this connection was that students in both schools could write to and for each other and that the teachers might share curriculum and ideas. Describing the entire project is beyond our scope here, but it is important to know a little of this history in understanding the production of the alphabet books as a critical literacy practice (see Comber 2004; Comber, Thomson & Wells 2002; Janks 2003). During the project our co-researcher, Pat Thomson, came across the picture alphabet book *A is for Aunty* (Russell 2000) and believed that it could generate some interesting work in both schools.

The book *A is for Aunty* deals with each letter of the alphabet through recounted memories of particular places, people and activities from an Aboriginal author and artist, Elaine Russell, especially of her life on an Aboriginal mission. For example, 'B is for Billycarts' tells how her brothers made billycarts out of old wooden boxes and wheels off old prams and painted them different colours. Many of the entries end with a short exclamatory sentence, such as: 'But it was great fun!' 'Fred's cart was the biggest and the fastest!' 'If we got tired of those games, we'd play hopscotch – for hours and hours!' The alphabet entries are illustrated beautifully with an emphasis on the place – the grass, river, sky, trees, dwellings and the people's activities in those spaces. In many ways this book can itself be seen as a counternarrative in that it provides a radical alternative to the often trite, frequently Anglo-cultural, white middle-class alphabet books available to many young children learning English worldwide. Russell's book also provides an account of the mission from her position as an Aboriginal child. Wells shared this book with her class, carefully attending to what Russell accomplished with her words and her art and inspiring them to write and illustrate *A is for Arndale*.

On first reading *A is for Arndale*, readers may assume that Wells' class had simply 'copied' the model of the genre and layout of *A is for Aunty* and reproduced that template with their own content. Indeed, innovating on story or generic structures is a popular way of scaffolding children's experiments with writing. While the children do appropriate key elements of the book's genre, style and design, a close reading of their texts indicate that they have clearly understood memory as a resource for narrative and the importance of specificity of places, people and activities. As we discuss, with examples below, the children were actively acquiring new discursive and semiotic resources for representing their lives.

It is not only reading and deconstructing Russell's text that has led to this development of a secondary discourse (Gee 1990). Wells had already undertaken a range of activities with her class to study the neighbourhood. They had created their own maps of the local area and studied street directories, scales and map co-ordinates (see Figure 7.1). They had undertaken planned walks of the neighbourhood noting changes relating to the Westwood redevelopment project. They had talked with the planners and developers about the actual designs and timelines for specific areas. They had undertaken research about the indigenous flora and fauna of the area to inform the plans for the new reserves. They had become involved in the proposal for a planned wetlands area. In other words, they had systematically been introduced to the discourses and practices of town planning and urban renewal. They had learnt to think of their places and dwellings in relation to the school, their classmates and the wider suburb. In their different excursions round the neighbourhood, they had photographed their own houses and others which were in various stages of demolition or renovation. On the computer some had redesigned their dwellings or designed 'dream houses' and structures of the future. Frequently urban renewal projects exclude or alienate the very people who are said to benefit (Arthurson 2001). However, in this case Wells makes a critical intervention. When these children came to write an alphabet book about their 'place', they had already thought, researched and studied their places – environmentally, as sites of pleasure, as architectural artefacts, as dangerous and more.

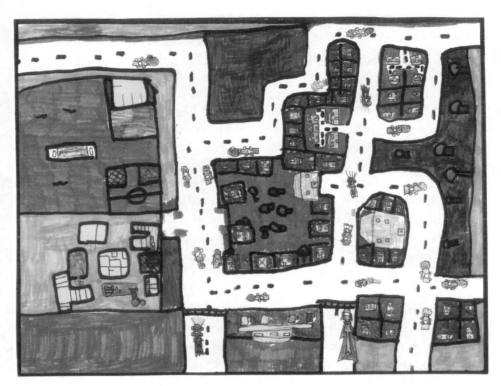

Figure 7.1 Map of local area

In many ways *A is for Arndale* was a text culminating from the children's substantial neighbourhood studies. Let us turn to the text itself as an instance of critical literacy practice. Like *A is for Aunty*, *A is for Arndale* represents a counternarrative in terms of the very context of its production. The alphabet book is one of the oldest technologies for teaching English literacy to children and here young children, working with the mediation and direction of their teacher and Elaine Russell's inspiration, produce an alphabet book significantly more complex than those typically designed and produced for children. Importantly they were producing this book not only for themselves and other classes at Ridley Grove Primary School, but also for young people at Paulina Sethole's school in South Africa (along with a companion volume, *Letters from Ridley*), so the quality of the presentation along with the clarity of their message were key. Their text needed to be able to 'speak for itself' as it spoke for them.

A is for Arndale is a 30-page, A3-size, colour illustrated alphabet book (with the 30 pages allowing each member of the class to produce a page and necessitating two entries for several letters). The front cover is a full-colour child-produced illustration of key places in the local area including the school, McDonalds, houses, parks and streets. Two introductory pages include a child-drawn aerial view of a part of the local area and an acknowledgement of Elaine Russell's inspirational text. The book itself then begins with 'A is for Arndale'. Arndale, as the child author explains, is 'a big shopping centre'. The writer goes on to inform the reader about the kinds of shops and restaurants at Arndale and finishes with personal preferences:

> I like looking at the CDs, the puppies in the pet shop, the rings in the jewellery shop and going into all the different stores.

This first entry introduces the reader to the key meeting place in this local area, and indeed in many places: the shopping mall. It also establishes a pattern followed by a number of the children of nominating a place (e.g. bike track, beach, catchment, hospital) and then introducing their preferred activities in that place, and the way their family does the particular activity. Other children foreground the activities, such as fishing or netball or rugby, then introduce the people and the places.

F
Is for Fishing

> Every holiday me and my dad go fishing. Sometimes we stay in a caravan and sometimes in a tent.
> Me and my dad cook dinner on an open fire. I love the squid. It is my favourite.
> My dad takes the black and white TV so we can watch it.
> We drive to Whyalla in the day time and we don't come back until night time.

The accompanying illustration depicts the tent, the ocean, the open fire, the dad and the writer. In each of the entries the children in one way or another describe a place which has significance for them and how they typically experience it. Another child explains at length how she, her mother and little brother 'do McDonalds' (along with details of Mum reading the newspaper), another how they visit the beach and yet another how they go to the movies (with the cousin separating brother and sister to avoid fights over popcorn). As is the case with Helen Grant's film-makers, Wells' class is encouraged to be ethnographers of everyday life. Their experiences become rich resources for meaning-making, in stark contrast to pervasive deficit discourses sometimes overheard in schools which contend that poor children have 'little or no experiences' (Comber 1998). Some children, like Elaine Russell, began to explore their lives in terms of specific memories of life's little incidents (see Figure 7.2).

I
Is for Ice Cream Van

> Every weekend the ice cream van drives around our streets selling ice creams.
> On Saturday, I hear it coming. It has a bell that rings. It's very old and has been coming around for as long as I can remember.
> When the van comes, I sometimes get an ice cream. My favourite is vanilla.
> Sometimes I am too late and miss the van and I chase after it. I cry if I miss the ice cream van. It comes on Sundays too, but I like to sleep in then.

Is for Ice Cream Van

Every weekend the ice cream van drives around our streets selling ice creams.

On Saturday, I hear it coming. It has a bell that rings. It's very old and has been coming around for as long as I can remember.

When the van comes, I sometimes get an ice cream. My favourite is vanilla.

Sometimes I am too late and miss the van and I chase after it. I cry if I miss the ice cream van. It comes on Sundays too, but I like to sleep in then.

Figure 7.2 I is for Ice Cream Van

In this and other entries we get a sense of the children living their lives, their pleasures and the contingency of those pleasures. Sometimes they get an ice cream, sometimes they get to buy a toy, sometimes they get to eat at McDonalds or buy rice crackers. The children's accounts of everyday life are fulsome and we believe indicate that they were acutely aware that they were writing this for other young people living somewhere else. Along with the many entries that are strongly infused with children's special pleasures (watching TV, playing sport or computer games, eating out, going to the movies and so on) are entries that focus on more troublesome aspects of their everyday lives in this locality. We hear of vandalised bike tracks, hospitals, busy roads, robberies, all narrated in a similarly understated way to how they write of their pleasures (see Figure 7.3):

> My house has TV's. We have two TV's. One TV is new and the other TV is broken, so I have to watch the new TV.

A little further on we read:

> On Friday my TV was stolen, so we called the police. We don't know who took the TV. My Mum got the old TV fixed and she bought us a new DVD.

In the entry for Q, 'Q is for quiet', the child writes:

> Around our neighbourhood it is usually noisy.
> Hanson Road is a very busy and noisy road. Lots of traffic goes up and down every day. There are lots of workers who work on the lights and snapped pipes.

Is for TV

My house has TV's. We have two TV's. One TV is new and the other TV is broken, so I have to watch the new TV.

I like the new TV too. I like to watch Cheez TV.

On Friday my TV was stolen, so we called the Police. We don't know who took the TV.

My mum got the old TV fixed and she bought us a new DVD.

Figure 7.3 T is for TV

> Some houses in our area are being knocked down and new ones being built. There are big bulldozers and cranes working all day.
> Some houses are very noisy and some are quiet. Neighbours sometimes have parties and they are very noisy. Sometimes it is hard to do your homework and get to sleep. It is best when it is really quiet.

Here we get some sense of the impact of the urban renewal project on the life of this child. Others write of noise too, and hair-raising attempts to cross the busy Hanson Road on their bicycles.

Other entries also show the impact of their neighbourhood studies and common neighbourhood events on children. One writes 'W is for Westwood', almost in the style of a press release genre, mentioning new trees and flowers that are part of the redevelopment (see Figure 7.4). Another writes knowledgeably and at length of the new catchment:

> Near our school, the Westwood people are making a park but it is not made yet. The park will have an Aboriginal theme with native plants and animals.
> We have been making new tiles for the park. These are going to be stuck on the seats.
> It will be very deep for the rainwater to be caught in the catchment area. There will be a small creek. The creek runs through the middle of the park.

The child goes on to explain the science behind the design of the catchment and some of the aesthetic elements of its design. As readers we found each of the entries

Is for Westwood

Westwood is the name of the new housing area being built near our school. There have been a lot of changes made.

Houses have been knocked down and new ones built. People are moving out and people are moving in. There are lots of new neighbours moved in already.

There's also new trees and flowers growing.

These changes will start closer to our school one day.

Figure 7.4   W is for Westwood

in this alphabet book incredibly interesting and the accompanying artwork at times troubling and at others uplifting. We cannot pretend to do this book justice here, but hope to give an inkling of what was being accomplished both pedagogically and materially.

Each child contributor to *A is for Arndale* gives a glimpse into life as they know it; some imagine what might be. Drawing on their individual and collective diverse resources, together they produce a text which becomes shared property and an important artefact within and beyond the school. At the very least all children and teachers at Ridley Grove Primary School would read their book. Their teacher and school principal were also taking it on a visit to Pauline Sethole's school in South Africa. From them, they anticipated and received a book in return, *A for Atteridgeville*. We consider the production of *A is for Arndale* as a critical literacy practice in this context because in the process children conducted complex analyses of life as they knew it in the changing circumstances of their locality. They assembled new narrative and representational resources to powerfully represent themselves and their peers. They redesigned the alphabet book from an adult, Western, white, normative technology of early literacy instruction, representing somebody else's world, to an inclusive, multi-vocal, contemporary text inviting conversation about their lives, cultures and times. They draw upon their knowledge of popular culture, their appropriation of the storytelling and artistic style of

Aboriginal author and painter, Elaine Russell, and their understandings of their neighbourhood to collectively produce an illustrated alphabet book that has become a favourite in the school and in the wider educational community in South Australia and beyond. The project continues. Recently Wells' class has learnt how to produce scaled drawings of their own houses. Wells, along with others who could be recruited to share their knowledge with the children (such as university architecture students, developers, journalists), is working to make available key spatial literacies which she believes are so important for her class.

Conclusion

In this chapter we have focused on the cultural re-reading as well as the re-writing and re-design that accompanied the co-production of texts by teachers and children in two critical literacy classrooms. We have reflected on classroom-produced texts because they serve as evidence of what can be accomplished materially by pedagogy. As texts, *A is for Arndale* and *Cooking Afghani Style* continue to have a material life in the classrooms and libraries of the two schools and in other places beyond. Since these texts were produced we have seen for ourselves how the children who made them still consult them and still claim them as 'their' book and 'their' film. In our view, both the process of making of the texts and the texts' materiality as physical objects performed important identity work for these children (Ormerod & Ivanic 2000). Not only did their teachers' neighbourhood curriculum and critical literacy pedagogy help the children to develop as individual literacy learners, they also enabled children to learn about each other and to work together as a collective to produce a book and a film that are valued and used by others. Finally, in each case the process of text production encouraged children to express both local and global commonalities as well as individual and cultural specificities. This is important social and cultural work which in these times is too rarely understood to be the domain of schooling in general and the English/literacy classroom in particular.

Implications for practice

Designing critical literacy curriculum in primary classrooms requires teachers to think about how to engage children in activities that focus on language and power. As well as understanding how other texts work, they need to learn how to make the texts that they produce have the desired effects in and on the world. When children are expert on their topics they can produce much more effective texts. Starting with their neighbourhoods is one way for children to begin to write powerfully.

- ● **Engage in an artefact audit of the texts produced in the classroom**

The aim is for teachers to reflect on whether and when the classroom is a place devoted to the production of purely 'functional' texts and whether and when it is devoted to the production of texts to which children, teachers and the community ascribe social and cultural value. This means valuing not only the operational aspects of texts such as decoding, but also the cultural, critical and perhaps emotional and aesthetic dimensions of texts. Below we list a number of questions that teachers might use to perform an 'artefact audit' of texts produced in their classrooms.

– What texts are produced in this classroom?

– What kinds of texts are children learning to be producers of?

– For what audience are these texts intended?

– Are these texts likely to be read or viewed? By whom?

– Whose voices and positions are represented in these texts and whose are absent?

– What investments do children and teachers have in these texts?

– What texts are children proud of? Which ones would children want to show others/keep/reread and review?

– How does the production of classroom texts involve children in assembling new knowledges and new semiotic resources?

– To what extent are children able to consider their own texts as cultural artefacts with specific local effects?

● Incorporate place-based activities in the literacy curriculum

We do not believe that the curriculum should be limited to the local. Indeed there are many arguments for children to be aware of an increasingly global community. However, beginning with events and sites in local neighbourhoods and communities ensures that all children have investments in the topics being studied. When assisted by their teachers they can also learn about the neighbourhood through new lenses. Such projects might include studying the diverse communities who inhabit the local neighbourhood now and in the past, particular places within the neighbourhood significant to different ethnic groups, local environmental issues such as the recycling of water, or local social issues such as the demolition of public housing.

● Develop a critical literacy approach to the reading and production of texts

To take a critical approach requires that teachers and children begin to closely examine the texts that they read and produce. In the neighbourhood, for example, teachers may begin by having children scrutinise the signs and billboards. Who is telling who to do what? Who is telling who about which products? Who is telling who about what not to do? Which signs welcome? Which signs bar? These everyday texts are an excellent place to begin to deconstruct how language works in the world. Children may then go on to look at the texts they produce in the same light. They may also decide to design alternate kinds of texts and representations that are more inclusive of the diversity of people who make up the audience for these signs and billboards.

References

Arthurson, K. (2001) 'Achieving social justice in estate regeneration: the impact of physical image construction', *Housing Studies*, 16 (6), 807–26.

Baker, C. & Davies, B. (1993) 'Literacy and gender in early childhood', in A. Luke & P. Gilbert (eds) *Literacy in contexts: Australian perspectives and issues*. Sydney: Allen and Unwin.

Comber, B. (1994) 'Critical literacy: an introduction to Australian debates and perspectives', *Journal of Curriculum Studies*, 26 (6), 655–68.

Comber, B. (1998) 'Problematising "background": (re)constructing categories in educational research', *Australian Educational Researcher*, 25 (3), 1–21.

Comber, B. (2001) 'Critical literacies and local action: teacher knowledge and a "new" research agenda', in B. Comber & A. Simpson (eds) *Negotiating critical literacies in classrooms*. Mahwah, NJ: Lawrence Erlbaum.

Comber, B. (2003) 'Critical literacy: what does it look like in the early years?' in N. Hall, J. Larson & J. Marsh (eds) *Handbook of research in early childhood literacy*. London: Sage/Paul Chapman.

Comber, B. (2004) 'Critical literacy educators at work: examining their dispositions, discursive resources and repertoires of practice', in R. White & K. Cooper (eds) *The practical critical educator*. The Netherlands: Kluwer Academic Publishers.

Comber, B. & Simpson, A. (eds) (2001) *Negotiating critical literacies in classrooms*. Mahwah, NJ: Lawrence Erlbaum.

Comber, B. Thomson, P. with Wells, M. (2001) 'Critical literacy finds a "place": writing and social action in a neighborhood school', *Elementary School Journal*, 101 (4), 451–64.

Comber, B., Thomson, P. & Wells, M. (2002) 'Critical literacy, social action and children's representations of "place".' Paper presented at the American Educational Research Association Annual Meeting, 1–5 April, 2002, New Orleans, Louisiana.

Department of Education, Training and Employment (2001) *South Australian curriculum, standards and accountability framework*. South Australia: DETE Publishing.

Fairclough, N. (ed.) (1992) *Critical Language Awareness*. London: Longman.

Freire, P. (1970) *Pedagogy of the oppressed*. New York: Herder & Herder.

Gee, J.P. (1990) *Social linguistics and literacies: ideology in discourse*. London: The Falmer Press.

Gilbert, P. (1991) 'Writing pedagogy: personal voices, truth telling and "real" texts', in C. Baker & A. Luke (eds) *Towards a critical sociology of reading pedagogy*. Amsterdam: John Benjamins.

Gruenewald, D. (2003) 'The best of both worlds: a critical pedagogy of place', *Educational Researcher*, 32 (4), 3–12.

Halliday, M. (1978) *Language as social semiotic: the social interpretation of language and meaning*. London: Edward Arnold.

Janks, H. (ed.) (1993) *Critical language awareness*. Johannesburg: Witwatersrand University Press and Hodder & Stoughton Educational.

Janks, H. (2000) 'Domination, access, diversity and design: a synthesis for critical literacy education', *Educational Review*, 52 (2), 175–86.

Janks, H. (2003) 'Seeding change in South Africa: new literacies, new subjectivities, new futures', in B. Doecke, D. Homer & H. Nixon (eds) *English teachers at work: narratives, counter narratives and arguments*. Adelaide: Australian Association of Teachers of English and Wakefield Press.

Kamler, B. (2001) *Relocating the personal: A critical writing pedagogy*. Albany: State University of New York Press.

Luke, A. (1996) 'Text and discourse in education: an introduction to critical discourse analysis', *Review of Research in Education*, 21, 3–48.

Luke, A. (2000) 'Critical literacy in Australia: a matter of context and standpoint', *Journal of Adolescent and Adult Literacy*, 43 (5), 448–61.

Luke, A., Comber, B. & Grant, H. (2003) 'Critical literacies and cultural studies', in G. Bull & M. Anstey (eds) *The literacy lexicon* (Second edition). Melbourne: Prentice-Hall.

Luke, A., Comber, B. & O'Brien, J. (1996) 'Critical literacies and cultural studies', in G. Bull & M. Anstey (eds) *The literacy lexicon*. Melbourne: Prentice-Hall.

Luke, A. & Freebody, P. (1999) 'Further notes on the four resources model', *Reading Online*, http//:www.readingonline.org/research/lukefreebody.htm.

McLaren, P. & Giroux, H. (1990) 'Critical pedagogy and rural education: A challenge from Poland', *Peabody Journal of Education*, 67 (4), 154–65.

Mellor, B., Patterson, A. & O'Neill, M. (1987) *Reading stories*. Perth: Chalkface Press.

New London Group (1996) 'A pedagogy of multiliteracies: designing social futures', *Harvard Educational Review*, 66 (1), 60–92.

Nixon, H. & Comber, B. (2004) 'Behind the scenes: making movies in early years classrooms', in J. Marsh (ed.) *Popular culture, media and digital literacies in early childhood*. London: RoutledgeFalmer.

O'Brien, J. (1994) 'Show mum you love her: Taking a new look at junk mail', *Reading*, 28 (1), 43–6.

O'Brien, J. (2001) 'Children reading critically: a local history', in B. Comber & A. Simpson (eds) *Negotiating critical literacies in classrooms*. Mahwah, NJ: Lawrence Erlbaum.

Ormerod, F. & Ivanic, R. (2000) 'Texts in practices: interpreting the physical characteristics of children's project work', in D. Barton, M. Hamilton & R. Ivanic (eds) *Situated literacies: Reading and writing in context*. London and New York: Routledge.

Russell, E. (2000) *A is for Aunty*. Sydney: Australian Broadcasting Corporation.

Searle, C. (1993) 'Words to a life-land: literacy, the imagination, and Palestine', in C. Lankshear & P. McLaren (eds) *Critical literacy: politics, praxis and the postmodern*. Albany: State University of New York Press.

Thomson, P. (2002) *Schooling the rustbelt kids: Making the difference in changing times*. Sydney: Allen & Unwin.

PART 3

Bridging the gap between children's personal interests and teachers' school-based curriculum demands

Educators are constantly trying to find ways of linking children's personal, out-of-school interests with the demands of the school curriculum. This last section looks at how these two demands can be 'fused' to the benefit of both the child and the teacher.

CHAPTER 8

Curiosity Kits:
Linking reading and play in the middle years

Ros Fisher

This chapter describes a project, Curiosity Kits, aimed at encouraging reluctant, mainly boy readers to read at home with other family members. The project has been successful in generating enthusiasm for reading and involving a wider range of family members in the reading that children bring from school. Particularly interesting has been the way children have been able to mix play with reading information texts. However, the question is raised as to how much room there is within the curriculum for playful encounters with text and even whether children see this as valuable.

Introduction

'New' in the context of literacy study recognises recent and novel forms of literacy but also implies new ways of looking at the familiar. Lankshear and Knobel (2003) classify the uses of the term 'new' as 'paradigmatic' and 'ontological' (p.16). The chapters in this book deal mainly with the ontological sense in which 'new' refers to the changes in the 'character and substance' of literacies associated with transformations in social practice. However, the paradigmatic shift from a way of looking at literacy that was largely based on psychology to a specific socio-cultural approach has also challenged existing orthodoxies about literacy and literacy teaching. Not only do teachers need to acknowledge and include new forms of literacy, they need to recognise new ways of looking at literacy practice. Literacy can no longer be considered mainly as a set of behaviours that inexperienced readers must master.

In classrooms in the UK, the USA and Australia recent initiatives are increasingly delineating the scope and purposes of literacy in school. The imperative to raise standards by ensuring children attain even more tightly prescribed levels has reduced the opportunity for play around texts. In this context, 'play' covers both 'games, exercise or other activity undertaken for pleasure, diversion etc. especially by children' and 'freedom of or scope or space for movement' (Collins 2003). As Luke (2003) argues:

> the classroom is one of the few places where formal taxonomic categories (e.g. the curriculum) and the official partitioning of time and space (e.g. the timetable) often are used to discourage children from blending, mixing, and matching knowledge drawn from diverse textual sources and communications media.
>
> (p. 398)

Curiosity Kits have proved to be one officially sanctioned way in which this blending can occur.

Curiosity Kits

Curiosity Kits were devised by Maureen Lewis in 1998 in response to a UK Government initiative to raise the profile of reading at home and in the community. Curiosity Kits are non-fiction book bags aimed to encourage boys and male family members to read at home. The kits were designed to motivate readers and to encourage wider participation in reading at home. For this reason the kit presents a broader definition of literacy than the normal 'reading book'. The basic 'kit' includes an information book on a topic of potential interest to boys, a magazine on a similar topic for adult family members, games and activities such as wordsearches, drawing or making projects, and a toy or artefact related to the topic.

For example, one kit had the *Flip Flap Body Book* (published by Usborne), a magazine called *Keep Fit*, an activity asking children to design a keep-fit machine, a model of the human body that could be taken apart and a wordsearch based on the text. Another had *The Young Athlete* (Dorling Kindersley), *Athletics Weekly*, a crossword puzzle, an activity to design a new super, streamlined bike, a puncture repair kit and racing gloves. The kits are kept in some form of sports bag such as a child might be keen to carry and not look like a school 'book bag'.

Since their inception, the idea has been developed in different ways appropriate to different contexts (Lewis & Fisher 2003). The original project was aimed at reluctant boy readers aged between seven and nine years. The evaluation showed that both parents and children enjoyed the kits; the number of books taken home increased; more members of the family were involved in shared readings – particularly more male family members; the games, activities and toys were enjoyed by the children; and teachers felt the kits were worthwhile and had had a beneficial effect on pupils' attitudes to reading (Lewis & Fisher 2001).

One of the interesting things to emerge from interviews with children in the original project was to do with the way some children talked about what they did when using the kits. One particularly interesting element was the relationship between the information book and the toy or artefact. One child told of the way he would read some of the book and then take the artefact and engage in fantasy play in a context arising from the text. Here he was able to make himself centre of the action of the play, informed by the text he was reading.

This mingling of private and public purposes for reading (Rosenblatt 1991) seemed a rich vein to explore with a view to understanding more about how children read non-fiction texts.

Play and literacy

The reading of non-fiction texts, although less widely covered than fiction, has received some attention in recent years. Whether from an information retrieval perspective, genre theory or critical literacy perspectives, the reading of non-fiction plays a growing part of literacy instruction in primary classrooms. In addition, it is often said that boys in particular enjoy reading information books, although evidence for this is weak and their motives challenged (Moss 2000). The Curiosity Kits project arose from this starting point. The Story Sacks project (Griffiths 2001) had been successful in developing younger children's reading but it was felt a project aimed particularly at motivating boys using non-fiction texts might be beneficial. The key element was that of motivation and the kits were designed with a view to promoting enjoyment of reading as well as involving other members of the family. As well as the books and magazines, the games and toys were seen to be crucial in encouraging children's engagement with these texts.

Rosenblatt (1991) identifies two possible stances that the reader can adopt: the efferent, in which the reader's predominant interest in the reading is to take away some information, and the aesthetic, in which the reader is more concerned with what s/he is thinking and feeling during the reading. In an efferent stance the reader's response is more related to public meanings, whereas an aesthetic stance relates more to the reader's private response. She argues that these two stances are not oppositional but dependent on individual ways of approaching text and our purposes when reading.

Rosenblatt and others (e.g. Holland & Shaw 1993; Fisher 1999) have further argued the role of the teacher in influencing the stances that children adopt when reading certain texts. It is important that teachers make sure that children do not automatically adopt a particular stance in response to a particular type of text. Rosenblatt (1991) expresses concern that current approaches to literacy teaching could exclude aesthetic responses through the mainly efferent use of texts as contexts for learning skills.

The relationship between play and literacy is not new although this has tended to centre on children playing at reading and writing, particularly in the early years. However, play also offers the opportunity for children to explore the meanings *they* identify in texts in their own individual way. Street (1984) argued that many schools adopt what he terms an 'autonomous' model of literacy in which literacy itself is an object to be studied and learnt rather than social practice which is shaped by those who use it. It is also argued that this 'autonomous' view of literacy disadvantages some children for whom the relationship between literacy practice at home and school literacy is not evident. Shannon (1990) argues that schools should encourage children to make sense of their experience by allowing them to develop their own voices. Christie (1998) states that critical theorists 'favour pedagogical approaches that give children control over their own literacy learning and that are closely linked to their own cultural experiences' (p. 51). The linking of play with the reading of information texts in Curiosity Kits potentially provides children with the opportunity to explore their own meanings through play.

What children say

In order to find out more about how children who use Curiosity Kits engage with the toys and artefacts, I went to a large primary school in the north of England where the kits had been in use for several years. The kits follow the pattern of the basic Curiosity Kit but do not contain a magazine for adults to go with the information book as it was found to be too expensive to keep these current.

Twenty-four children were interviewed, representing all those who were in school on the day of my visit and who had taken part in the Curiosity Kits project over the previous year. The interviews were conducted in groups of three or four children and followed a semi-structured format.

Interview questions:

1   What do you like best about Curiosity Kits? Why?
2   Tell me about how you used them.
3   Which was your favourite?
4   Did you like having a toy?
5   What did you do with it? Did you make up stories?
6   Do you think the Curiosity Kits helped your reading? How?
7   Did having the toy help at all?

In the first instance the interview had been designed to explore the use of props in the Curiosity Kits to support fantasy play. However, early on in the interviews it became clear that play, as part of using a Curiosity Kit, covered more types than just fantasy play. For this reason, questions 4 and 5 became more wide-ranging and followed up on what children had said about how they used the kits, including playing with the games and puzzles as well as the toy or artefact.

Almost without exception, children said it was the games and activities that they enjoyed. They mentioned making things, for example, a dinosaur out of construction straws; playing games, such as a game with stars; investigations, such as looking at insects through a magnifying glass. Fun seemed to be a clear factor. One girl reflected the view of many when she repeated several times that they were not boring: 'It's just great fun. You get to play loads and loads of games and make stuff.' Some children, but only when prompted, could talk about making up stories with the toys. They spoke of 'making the dinosaurs stomp around' and of fights between bugs or dinosaurs.

The responses from children in relation to their play activities while using the Curiosity Kits fell into three broad categories:

- reality-oriented play such as games, puzzles and making models;
- imaginative play;
- school-oriented responses.

These categories were not mutually exclusive. Nearly all children spoke enthusiastically of the puzzles, games and making activities. About half also told of stories they had made up based on the topic of the information book and the toys or artefacts contained in the kit. These imaginative play responses fell into a further three categories:

- fantasy play (general);
- fantasy play (based on themes from popular culture);
- play scenarios based on the child's own life experience.

Reality-oriented play such as games, puzzles and making models

The opening question about Curiosity Kits asked children if they remembered using Curiosity Kits and what they liked about them. This was clearly a leading question but nearly all children responded enthusiastically to the mention of Curiosity Kits and warmed to the topic as the interview proceeded. Those few children who were less than enthusiastic will be discussed later. In the first instance, children referred to the games, to making things and to the activities. Those who responded initially in a more general way said they were 'fun' and then went on to describe which games or activities were fun.

The kind of activities that children enjoyed varied. Many children mentioned making a picture of a dinosaur from paper construction straws and making a model of a pyramid. Another popular kit included a magnifying glass with plastic insects. Several children talked about looking at the insects through the magnifying glass. A few children particularly mentioned games which they could play with other members of the family. There were children whose self-chosen activity was more factually based. One boy enjoyed matching the dinosaur models with the pictures in the book.

Imaginative play

It proved much more difficult to get children to talk about whether they played or made up stories with the toys or artefacts that were included in the kits. Only after probing did some children tell about how they played with the toys. Below I speculate on how much this may be to do with the expectations children have about 'school work' and 'play'. In the end 13 of the 24 children could talk about a story they had made up based on the Curiosity Kits. Of these, seven were boys and six were girls.

Fantasy play (general)

Mostly it seems, in children's memories at least, the stories were not fully developed. One boy said he made the dinosaurs 'stomp around' and another that he chased his sister with the bugs. The 'Dinosaurs', 'Insects' and 'Egyptian' kits gave rise to most of the fantasy play – mostly of a violent kind. Some children were able to describe their play in more detail:

'I make up stories where a dinosaur kills another one. A great big one rips the other one.' (Boy)

'I did an Egyptian one with all the Egyptians dying.' (Boy)

'I made up a story called "Bug to the Rescue".' (Girl)

'I imagined I was in a dinosaur land with all the dinosaurs around me. They was trying to get me and eating me.' (Girl)

Fantasy play (based on themes from popular culture)

It was also marked that often the themes from the Curiosity Kits linked with themes from popular culture and that both elements fed into children's fantasy play.

'There's a dragon and it eats people up – like Jurassic Park.' (Girl)

'I made one up with that beetle – that it was . . . like scarabs do with the mummy.' (Boy).

He then moved into the story from the film 'The Mummy' and discussed this and other films with the children in the group. They made clear links between the bug in 'The Matrix' and with bugs in general.

Play scenarios based on the child's own life experience

Other children seemed to use play to explore their own life experiences through the themes of the Curiosity Kits. My favourite was the girl who described a story related to the Insect pack in which a ladybird had a baby. When I looked surprised, she giggled with embarrassment and explained that she had a four-month-old brother who was there while she was playing with the Curiosity Kits. A boy described how he had put the bugs into a bug hospital with 'stuff collected from around the house'. A girl who had had a Transport pack said, 'I went to the garage and my dad bought me a car and I went wheeee all round the garden!'

School-oriented responses

Just five children, four girls and a boy, said they did not play with the toys or make up stories. The boy said, 'I did play with them but not in the sort of way you are thinking of. I just played with them like the Curiosity Kit said.' There is a sense in these children's answers that they did not see the Curiosity Kits as being for play. One girl who enjoyed the colouring and drawing in the kits said she did not imagine anything in relation to the toys and added, 'There's not even things about doing stuff with it' (referring to a particular toy). This suggests that she saw the kits as a form of homework in which there are given activities to undertake. Indeed several children when talking about the activities used language such as 'you have to . . .' For example, 'What you have to do is . . . You had a magnifying glass and you had to look at them and sketch them – there were ladybirds and grasshoppers.' This type of language does not necessarily imply constraint but set alongside those children who chose not to play it raises questions about whether those children see reading primarily as a task/school-oriented activity in which someone else defines what you do.

Discussion

It seems from the brief glimpse afforded by these children that the play that arose from Curiosity Kits was essentially different from Rowe's (2000) definition of book-related play. Rowe defines this as 'involving symbolic transformations that explicitly or implicitly reflect the meanings signed in text or illustrations, or in the book reading events in which children encounter books' (p. 4). The play events that arose from these children's use of Curiosity Kits did not seem exactly to 'reflect the meanings signed in text or illustrations' but rather to develop from an inner response, in which children made connections from the content of the text with their own lives. Thus the meanings arising from the texts were personal and individual to each child rather than necessarily arising from the author's meanings as Rowe's definition could imply.

It was perhaps surprising that these children did not make explicit links to the books from their play, although this study arose from the comments of one child who did just that. It was only when prompted that any child spoke of having the toys to hand when they were reading. One child who had talked of liking the stethoscope in the Body kit was unable to say whether stethoscopes were shown in the text. Rather the movement seemed from the books into the play, perhaps providing the opportunity for children to move out from their reading as opposed to it being bounded by school-based interpretations. Thus no claims can be made for a direct relationship between the toy and reading comprehension (or learning facts), although some children said they thought this was an important benefit of the kits. Furthermore, much of the play described by children was of a violent kind, usually very fanciful, often undeveloped and sometimes linked to themes from popular culture.

There are two possible types of response to these findings. The first type will come from the teacher who is anxious to provide effective learning situations with recognisable outcomes. His/her response will be to say that more direction is needed or even that the toys and artefacts are an unnecessary part of the kit (as some teachers have done). The second type of reaction will be from the teacher who sees a benefit in the very fact that responses are varied and variable. S/he will not mind that they are more related to the child's personal responses than a measurable increase in reading attainment. S/he will argue that the opportunity for the child to develop and explore his/her own interpretations is valuable in its own right and can lead, potentially, to even more valuable outcomes in terms of motivation and understanding.

The lack of a clear linear connection between play and learning should not be seen as an argument that the toys and artefacts are an unimportant part of the Curiosity Kit. Indeed, it seems to me that what is important is this very freedom for children to explore, *in the way that is relevant to them*, the ideas that arise from the text. Too often children's responses to texts are controlled by the teacher's agenda and by a need to meet targets.

Increasingly, the discourse of schooling separates learning from life. Schools need to make explicit how children are progressing. Measurable evidence of gains and clearly defined outcomes are paramount. Both teachers and children are clear that success in assessment situations is important for success in school. What may be less clear to children is how success in school relates to their personal experience. Alvermann and Hagood (2000) argue that:

> [s]chool design, pedagogical implementation, and relations between teachers and students highlight distinctions between work and pleasure, classroom and playground, in-school and out-of-school literacies, teacher and student, and mind and body within school discourse.

> (p.199)

As mentioned earlier, Rosenblatt (1991) argues that both public and private responses to literacy should be developed. She reminds us that psychologists have pointed out that:

> connections between the verbal signs and what they signify involve both what the words are understood to refer to (their public, dictionary meaning) and the feelings,

ideas and attitudes (their private associations) that have become linked with them through past reading or life experiences.

(pp. 445–6)

Through their simple and undeveloped exploration of the meanings that *they* identified, some of these children were able to mix public and private interpretations, school and home literacy experiences. It is arguably of more concern that a few children were not able to do this (or not willing to reveal this to me – a school-based adult). What are their understandings of literacy that they did not want to go beyond the defines of the school task?

Although criticisms can be made of the 'old-style transmission and surveillance pedagogy' (Luke 2003), we cannot ignore children's complicity in this. The question as to the extent to which teachers should intervene in the play element of children's reading is moot. Undoubtedly, without the toy some children would have played anyway. By providing a toy, it seemed that, for some children, teachers were giving permission to play. For those children who did not use the toy because they did not see it as a required part of the kit, might it have been useful to direct children to the toys through discussion of how other children have used them? Whether more direction with the dinosaurs would have improved the quality of play or inhibited children's response because of the direction is a difficult question to answer.

Certainly it seems from this small-scale study that there is scope for children beyond the very early years to have opportunities to play with and around the themes of literacy. If children are to establish their own links between content, task and meanings, they need the freedom to do this. Too often literacy in the school context is constrained by other people's conceptions of what literacy should be and what it is for. It has already been shown that school views of literacy dominate the home context (Kelly *et al.* 2002). Perhaps these children's enjoyment of games, puzzles and fantasy play around information books provides a small opportunity for home conceptions of meaning to infiltrate schooled literacy.

Implications for practice

● **Consider ways of encouraging play around texts**

This can be through drama improvisations, art, music or other ways of allowing a variety of responses to texts – both fiction and non-fiction. Reconsider the opportunities children have for play – are there occasions when toys, games or artefacts could be used?

● **Value children's home reading interests in school**

Evaluate your response to children's own texts and their interpretations of texts, from home or school. Is there the possibility for engagements with texts to be fun?

Do you allow your genuine concern to meet targets to override your own enthusiasm for reading?

Find out how to set up a Curiosity Kit scheme

Think about how you could link children's home and school reading in a way that goes beyond providing school-directed tasks to be completed at home. For details of Curiosity Kits, go to:

http://sellweb.ex.ac.uk/~rjf201/curiositykits/teacherleaflet.doc.

References

Alvermann, D.E. & Hagood, M.C. (2000) 'Critical Media Literacy: Research, Theory and Practice in "New Times" ', *Journal of Educational Research*, 93, 193–205.

Christie, J.F. (1998) 'Play as a Medium for Literacy Development', in D.P. Fromberg & D. Bergen (eds) *Play from Birth to Twelve and Beyond: Contexts, Perspectives, and Meanings*. London: Taylor and Francis.

Collins (2003) *English Dictionary* (Sixth edition). Glasgow: HarperCollins.

Fisher, R. (1999) 'When is a story not a story?', *Education 3–13*, 27 (1), 18–23.

Griffiths, N. (2001) *Story Sacks*. Reading: Reading and Language Information Centre.

Holland, K.E. & Shaw, L.A. (1993) 'Dances between Stances', in K.E. Holland, R.A. Hungerford & S.B. Ernst (eds) *Journeying: Children responding to literature*. Portsmouth, NH: Heinemann.

Kelly, C., Gregory, E. & Williams, A. (2002) 'A new understanding of family involvement', in R. Fisher, G. Brooks & M. Lewis (eds) *Raising Standards in Literacy*. London: Falmer 66–81.

Lankshear, C. & Knobel, M. (2003) *New Literacies: Changing Knowledge and Classroom Learning*. Buckingham: Open University Press.

Lewis, M. & Fisher, R. (2001) 'Curiosity Kits', *Topic: Practical Applications of Research in Education*, Spring Issue.

Lewis, M. & Fisher, R. (2003) *Curiosity Kits*. Reading: National Centre for Language and Literacy.

Luke, C. (2003) 'Pedagogy, connectivity, multimodality, and interdisciplinarity', *Reading Research Quarterly*, 38 (3), 397–403.

Moss, G. (2000) 'Raising boys' attainment in reading', *Reading*, 34 (4), 101–6.

Rosenblatt, L.M. (1991) 'Literature – S.O.S.' *Language Arts*, 68, October.

Rowe, D.W. (2000) 'Bringing Books to Life: The Role of Book-Related Dramatic Play in Young Children's Literacy Learning', in K.A. Roskos & J.F. Christie (eds) *Play and Literacy in Early Childhood*. Mahwah, NJ: Lawrence Erlbaum Associates.

Shannon, P. (1990) *The struggle to continue: Progressive reading instruction in the United States*. Portsmouth, NH: Heinemann.

Street, B. (1984) *Literacy in Theory and Practice*. Cambridge: Cambridge University Press.

Writing about heroes and villains

Fusing children's knowledge about popular fantasy texts with school-based literacy requirements

Elaine Millard

It is important that as educationalists we regularly re-examine our fixed certainties about the values embedded in the curriculum choices we make and the resources we teach them, by submitting both to rigorous review. This chapter describes how one teacher worked to develop competent, critical and engaged readers. In particular it focuses on how she re-examined the role that books, particularly those designated in the curriculum as 'literature' or with 'literary merit', might play in the curriculum. It argues the case for fusing the concerns of popular culture with the teaching of classic works of children's literature, widening teachers' critical understanding of multi-modality in the creation of fantasy. Further, it suggests that there is a role for teacher educators and researchers to support teachers in their struggle to make increasingly regulated curricula their own to the benefit of their children.

Introduction

Children's literature has, like apple pie and motherhood, been considered a staple of Western culture and its use in school therefore deemed to bring only positive outcomes for teaching and learning. Implicit in the prescription of specific works or authors for reading in schools is the view that reading can make us better people by developing a greater sensitivity to the world we live in and the lifestyles we aspire to. It is a view that is promoted by Valentine Cunningham, Senior English Tutor at Corpus Christi College, Oxford, in his contribution to a collection of essays on the importance of reading entitled *Literacy Is Not Enough* (Cox 1998) in which he argues for the separation of literary studies (good) from a focus on literacy (bad).

Even when researchers are committed to the power of popular culture, they often continue to insist on the importance of a book's literary qualities, as is shown in the conclusion to the following quotation from research which argues for the importance of the folk tale:

> What are needed are beginning texts that fascinate children and convince them that reading both is delightful and helps one to gain a better understanding of oneself and others – in short, of the world we live in and of how to live in it. To achieve this, primary texts should stimulate and enrich the child's imagination, as fairy tales do, and should develop the child's literacy sensitivities, as good poems are apt to do. *The texts should also present the child with literary images of the world, of nature and of man, as these have been created by great writers* [my added emphasis].

> (Bettleheim & Zelan 1982: 263)

In terms of school provision, literary value is often attributed only to those books that focus on psychological realism and many teachers set great store by the power of 'good' literature to teach about the people and events of the real world. Hence the repeated moral panics associated with children's books and recognised 'quality' authors who dare to deal with difficult subjects like teenage sex (Judy Blume's *Forever*) or drugs (Melvin Burgess's *Junk*). Often left unexplored is the way in which readings of all manner of texts other than books, such as, for example, televisual, film, comic strip and digital images, build towards a deeper understanding of the way in which language constructs new meanings and how narrative forms in different modalities may support one another. These aspects then, the power of story and its role in developing understanding about how language creates a range of realities, are the important issues informing this chapter.

The role of book fantasies in reading development

First, it is important to revisit the claims made for books which are still the staple of narrative and reading in school. In a recent essay, *Happy Ever After*, published in the *Guardian Saturday Review* and adapted from the introduction to *The Annotated Brothers Grimm* (Tatar 2004), the novelist A.S. Byatt (2004) writes of her earliest experiences of fantasy narratives. She recounts the pleasures she derived from all manner of folk and fairy tales, which she read 'voraciously and indiscriminately'. These she calls 'wonder tales' and argues that the fascination of such stories for her and other children lies not in any insight they afford into human nature but rather in their very refusal of this. It was not psychological realism she craved from her early encounters with stories but, as she explains, their power to astonish: 'I never really liked stories about children, doing what children do – quarrelling and cooking and camping. I liked magic, the unreal, the more than real' (p. 4).

Francis Spufford (2002), who has written a memoir of the history of his own childhood reading in *The Child That Books Built*, writes similarly of the earliest phase of his reading, approving its lack of detailed characterisation:

In true fairy tales, as opposed to literary hybrids, smuggling in the techniques of the novel, there are no individual characters – only types. Good princess; bad princess . . . the vocabulary of types is actually easier to acquire than knowledge about the child's own world.

(p. 50)

Byatt and Spufford also agree about the next stage of their literary involvements and describe how as child readers they became increasingly involved in the narrative through identification with its central characters. Spufford recalls reliving the action of Middle Earth through the eyes of Bilbo Baggins, while Byatt fell in love with Sir Launcelot and Arthurian legend. Both describe the alternative worlds provided by their books as a way of extending their own possible roles, as a form of play, delighting in action and make-believe, rather than revealing truths or any lessons to be learnt.

The educationalist J. Appleyard has systemised such personal accounts of reading development more deliberately in his academic account of *Becoming a Reader* (1990). He attributes a sequence of stages to the acquisition of the reading habit from childhood to adulthood. He argues that each stage provides an advance on the way of thinking about a story and sees the individual reader, irrespective of background or personality, as progressing from an early absorption with fantasy play world, through identification with central characters, to a more critical and analytical stage that allows one to stand back and make judgements. He labels the first stage as 'Reader as Player' in which the young reader dwells in the story as one of the various characters. This, he suggests, is not simply a question of the child reimagining or reinventing the story; but a means whereby they re-enact fictional events in a very active and participatory manner. Appleyard's categories, which derive from a Piagetian concept of necessary stages, are indeed too rigidly sequential to encompass the wide range of experiences that all children derive from their reading. However, his categories, though idealised, are helpful in understanding the way in which story can capture a child's imagination as portrayed by the two previous creative writers.

All three, Byatt, Spufford and Appleyard, share a privileged entrance to children's books, literature and later professional literary pursuits through induction in their early years into a book-dominated culture. Their precious early experiences laid the firm foundation for later imaginative involvement with fiction. Indeed, literacy researchers have frequently reported that early encounters with story can be powerful predictors of children's later success within the school systems of Western cultures (Wells 1987) and that no bedtime story can spell failure for children who come from a more oral tradition or one where fiction is treated with suspicion as not conveying spiritual truths (Heath 1983). Imaginative fiction has been placed at the heart of most early learning programmes and it is a curricular imperative for English teachers in Western cultures that their students should read widely and be well informed about books and authors. What 'reading' widely and being well informed might mean in the twenty-first century is the issue I now want to consider more critically.

Children's understanding of fantasy in narrative

For many children, the established house of fiction in schools can seem a more alien and for some, even a threatening place, that bears no resemblance to their own home experience or familial social and cultural capital (Bourdieu 1984). Even where books are a key part of home experience, the books children choose and enjoy may not be those that are chosen as 'quality texts' in school (Moss 1977; Wilkinson 2003). Wilkinson, in fact, found that in the reading of four pre-school children, one of whom had a mother committed to the notion of 'quality' in her child's reading, only 'four of the thirteen favourite books could be said to fall within the established canon of children's literature' (Wilkinson 2003: 297). The mismatch between the personal pleasures of home and the demands of school prescription can easily quell early enthusiasms. For example, the children's author Michael Morpurgo recently told teachers at the 2004 conference of National Association for the Teaching of English (NATE) that school had made him anxious about writing and for a while had seriously dampened the enthusiasm he had formed for storying from his mother's readings of children's classics. How much more daunting school must then be for children where print narrative is not the main narrative medium shared by parent and child. As Marsh (2004) found in a study of early literacy experiences in the home, many children are introduced to narrative and its goodies and baddies through media other than continuous prose narrative. The characters and the trajectory of their stories are more frequently accessed through such visual media as comic strips, TV series, films, usually in the home on DVD and video, and the ubiquitous battles of villains, monsters and adventurers of computer games. Moreover, many of the books that are chosen for them are spin-offs from such media representations of stories, such as *The Little Mermaid* and *Bob the Builder*.

There is a tendency among many teachers to see these developments as an impoverishment of the child's imaginative world and a distraction from the 'real' reading curriculum. It is also often the case that television and computer games are thought to compete with the child's reading experiences rather than to enlarge and develop them (Marsh & Millard 2000). Lambirth (2003), who surveyed the attitudes to popular culture of 65 teachers involved in an LEA writing project, found that:

> Teachers demonstrated a rather ambivalent stance towards popular culture, on the one hand speaking with warmth and affection of their own childhood encounters with popular texts, on the other indicating revulsion for contemporary popular culture.

(p. 9)

The American researcher Seiter (1999) identified two kinds of teacher response to their classes' popular interests; the first is where children are viewed as passive victims who need protection from the ravages of media, the second views them as the active constructors of meaning in their world. In British culture the former is the most commonly held view of primary teachers who are reported as generally thinking that their children were exposed to enough of their own popular cultural interests at home and it had no place in their school curriculum (Lambirth 2003).

It seems that many teachers regret the perceived loss of a richness of language and verbal play, which they assume comes from the printed word, so they attempt to exclude the products of children's culture from their classrooms and more specifically from their English lessons. However, as Dyson (1997, 2000, 2003) has shown, maintaining such exclusions in school is an impossible task as the children conspire to smuggle their obsessions into their school writing as well as into their lockers. She describes how they recontextualise the stuff of home and community and use popular texts to construct bridges between official and unofficial worlds, showing vividly how children deploy their own textual 'stuff' to 'amuse, please or just pass muster' as she works 'to place childhoods themselves center stage in the study of literacy development' (Dyson 2000: 34). As she comments:

> Children draw deeply upon non-academic social worlds to negotiate their entry into school literacy; those worlds provide them with agency and meaningful symbols, including those from popular music, films, animated shows and sports media.
>
> (Dyson 2000: 15)

However, most teachers remain very resistant to children's use of popular culture and non-academic material in their school work and it has been argued that because of this hostility children may find the literacy practices of school increasingly arid and meaningless (Pennac 1994; Hilton 1996), or divorced from the practices of their communities and cultures (Marsh & Millard 2000). Moreover, there is some evidence that the current incorporation of new literacies into schooled practices only works to render them both ineffective and meaningless as forms of communication (see for example Lankshear *et al.* 1997 on the use of email as a school exercise).

Researching children's interests

Because of my perception of the continuing mismatch between children's experiences and desires and their teachers' drive to produce critical and engaged readers, I have in the past five years undertaken a series of small-scale projects directed at merging what at first may appear to be the contradictory impulses of working with children's culture and developing an enthusiasm for the literacy activities demanded by set curricula. These have involved children creating their own class comic, creating story maps and using PowerPoint to explore and develop narrative effects as well as drawing and designing places and characters for their own stories and plays. This experience has confirmed my view that children can find more continuities and correspondences in the narrative worlds of the televisual and print texts than contradictions and discontinuities, no more so than in the primary stages of becoming a reader where heroes and villains stalk every path or corridor of the dark woods and enchanted palaces of the imagination. A popular film like *Shrek* (Dreamworks 2001), with its multiple references to both fairy tales and classic literature such as *Don Quixote*, is a prime example of how each medium borrows, builds on and transforms previous narrative traditions. Not only this, but it then also adds to the possible reading diet a whole range of print spin-offs and factual as well as fictional texts. A current search of the Amazon site revealed 52 book-based spin-offs from this single movie.

The projects were conducted with classes of eight-, nine- and ten-year-old children. The emphasis was on 'fusing' the children's current interests with their teachers' school-based planning and on valuing their contributions and their growing understanding of what makes a story work (Millard 2003a). Fusion suggests a melding of the disparate elements in which each component is able to make an important contribution to the developing narrative. The teachers' role is central in facilitating the children's freedom to move between different types of text, making connections and pondering differences (Millard, 2003a & 2003b). Teachers are also crucial in creating appropriate opportunities to give access to the fantasy genre and in exploiting the affordances of each mode of communication. It requires both confidence in their own teaching and an awareness of children's understandings; a teaching quality which is popularly described as 'child-centred' but which Bruner (1999) has termed 'mutualist'. It involves 'an exchange of understanding between the teacher and the child' and the ability 'to find in theintuitions of the child the roots of systematic knowledge' (Bruner 1999: 57). Wells, speaking from a Vygotskian perspective, reminds us that, 'the first and most important concern must be to ensure that reading and writing are undertaken for some purpose that is of significance to the learner' (Wells 2003: 191). Rebecca Jurd, the teacher involved in each of the projects, had just such motivations and confidence and was happy to experiment with a project based on children's out-of-school interests.

Introducing popular fantasy narratives in class

In, our first project, The Castle of Fear, (Millard in press), a class of 35 eight- and nine-year-olds were asked to write a problem-solving adventure story in which they adopted the role of a gamester or adventurer, who had been set a task to accomplish in the face of dire dangers. To assist their planning, they were given a sheet of A3 paper folded into three so that the front represented the opening of a castle. Once opened, the inside sheet was divided into a number of rooms, each designed to contain an individual threat and its possible solution (see Figures 9.1(a) & (b) and 9.2(a) & (b)).

Figure 9.1(a) Girl's exterior plan for the castle. The colours chosen for this were predominantly pastel shades of pink and green

Rebecca and I jointly planned a series of lessons, each focused on particular aspects of the writing process, such as a general introduction for the reader, descriptions of settings and the main characters, and solutions to the problems. The children drew readily from a wealth of implicit knowledge about how such stories are framed. The simple castle map we provided, represented in another form the structure of a computer game's alternative routes to a solution.

The children took their heroes and villains from all manner of sources, including comic book heroes, videos of Disney, adaptations of fairy tales, information about these on the web, television series and stories they had encountered in school. Popular stories adapted for film such as *Harry Potter and the Philosopher's Stone* or *The Lord of the Rings* featured prominently. There was even a visual cue taken from the film *Chocolat* which a girl had been allowed to watch with her mother.

Rebecca had also added sections from *The Hobbit*, which she had chosen to read as the class novel, as a stimulus for discussion leading on to the forms of writing

Figure 9.1(b) Girl's interior showing the kangaroo motif taken from the film *Chocolat*. Note the same pastel colours are used as for the exterior

that we hoped to develop. One such piece of writing was an imitation of the opening of the book in which Bilbo Baggins' hole is described by means of antonyms (what it was not like). The children had practised describing their classroom in these terms with some success as is shown in the following examples. Miss Jurd's class was:

> . . . not a fancy classroom with the smell of a thousand dogs. It is not a peaceful classroom at all. It is not colourful. It was class Jurd and that means friendship and laughter.
>
> . . . not a dark gloomy sort of a place that smelled of a foul pair of trainers and sweaty PE shirts. This was class Jurd and that meant peace and warmth.
>
> . . . not a dirty scruffy classroom that smells like smelly feet that have not been washed. The wallpaper was not drizzling off the walls. It was class Jurd and that means fun and friends.
>
> . . . not an ordinary classroom. It was a machinery classroom with easy chairs. There was a doughnut shop for lunch. All doughnuts are free. The machinery has help for

Figure 9.2(a) A boy's exterior, coloured red and black

anything you need. It knows your age and sex. It was class Jurd and that means fun. [This from a child with special needs and support help.]

Other shared writing activities had been based on the conversation of the 'Trolls in the Roast Mutton' chapter of the book. This is clearly echoed in the composition of one boy, usually most noted for not wanting to write:

Monster Argument

'What are we going to do with him wandering around?'
'Boil him,' said the man called Batty.
'We've got no water,' whispered Lesley.
'The lakes a long way – there's no way I'm going there!'
'Well sit on him,' whispered Lesley.
'No way! He might bite my bottom and it's still sore from the last boy we had.'
'We ended up letting that last boy go,' said Lesley, sadly.

This piece with the slightly transgressive 'bite my bottom' was readily enacted by others in his group to the amusement of the class.

A group collaboration using the pattern of language taken from the first encounters with Gandalf where Bilbo extols the magician's reputation by repeating the phrase 'Not the . . .', produced the following joint text, based on their chosen popular hero, Harry Potter:

Figure 9.2(b) Boy's interior plan for inside the castle

Not *the Harry Potter* who lives with the Dursley family at 4 Privet Drive.
Not that boy with the round glasses who goes to Hogwart's School for magicians and is famous for his skill at Quidditch.
Not *the lad* who can perform such clever magic and owns an owl called Hedwig.
Not *the rascal* who magicked a tail on his cousin.
Not *the brave investigator* who found the Chamber of Secrets.
Not the *son of Lilly Potter*.

Making the most of collaborative talk

As we returned to review the children's narrative constructions at the close of the project, Rebecca and I judged that we had promoted and encouraged talk in a wide range of registers. Moreover, wherever the literary stimulus provided for shared writing had been taken up in their stories, they had been able to give more force to describing the elements taken from their own preferred texts. It was also clear that many children who had difficulty in writing at length had experienced no difficulty in constructing their adventures visually, using their maps for elaborate retellings whenever they were invited to share their stories.

The original project had helped Rebecca to link key aspects of the children's chosen worlds with their symbolic identities to inform and motivate the development of focused literacy work (Millard in press). It had also allowed both of us to investigate the powerful gender messages that helped the children to position themselves in relation to others (Gilbert 1992). Discussions of gendered differences in the choice of characters and actions had been a key part of the work of sharing and developing the stories. In the next stage of the project, which was to be a six-week block, we agreed to focus more directly on those elements that had produced the most extended writing for all the children. We decided to build the narrative around a classic work of fiction and we settled on *The Lion, the Witch and the Wardrobe*, as a story with a very strong fantasy theme. Into this work we chose to introduce other modes of creating stories using story mapping, video reproductions and information researched on the Internet. Instead of a story map, we created a little chapter book with writing prompts at the head of each section which the children were encouraged to view as interconnected chapters. There were six sections based on the structure of a simple narrative with an opening descriptive section, a new world entered, a complication, a struggle with an enemy and a peaceful resolution. The following prompts are from the two central complication sections:

> Chapter 3: There is a task to complete. The children need to find their way through the enemy's territory. Describe what they see on the way and the objects they find.
> Chapter 4: The enemy is waiting outside. Describe what they look like and what they are planning to do.

Each section was composed in a separate session of approximately 40 minutes, preceded by a 20-minute shared class reading or writing activity.

When 'teaching' the structure and affordances of fantasy stories we first introduced *The Lion, the Witch and the Wardrobe* using the section describing the transformation from the interior of the wardrobe to the cold of the land that is forever winter. We made feely boxes containing leaves, twigs, pebbles, silk and velvet to help the children to describe different settings such as a forest or wood, a beach and a palace which they might use in their own stories. They brainstormed a wide range of descriptive phrases and then in pairs they analysed the text, picking out specific appeals to the senses, such as:

> Feeling the hard smooth wood of the floor ... something soft and powdery and extremely cold; no longer soft fur, but something hard and rough and prickly.

Ways of structuring children's narrative

The children were then asked to begin to plan their stories, using a range of devices incorporating mapping, drawing and writing. Their first task was to design the magic entrance to their individually devised fantasy worlds by sketching an imaginary wardrobe, cupboard, garage or toy box, whose doors or lid would give access to the imagined world. As with the Castle of Fear, a folded A3 sheet was used to produce the opening onto a map of the chosen world. Discussion followed concerning creating themed names for places. For example, a girl who had chosen the Land of Sweets for her fantasy world had names such as the Lollipop Forest, the Coca-Cola Lake and the Fizzy Pop Volcano, while a boy had chosen Skeleton Island, Graveyard Woods and Murky River for his Spooky Land. Next came more shared writing to expand on the descriptive detail of the setting from the lists of sensory words made with the feely boxes. This gave an opportunity to discuss onomatopoeia and alliteration with descriptive choices such as 'crisp, crunchy snow', 'soft, sifting sand' and 'round, smooth pebbles'.

Using the affordances of film

The next episode we focused on was the arrival of the White Witch and a description of her manner. The children read the text and then watched a video version, noting aspects of her appearance and behaviour. The class was asked to think of any villains who had scared or amazed them in the stories they had read or seen. The list, as on previous occasions when working on the Castle of Fear, was dominated by current film and television productions. The character most cited was Voldemort ('he who must not be named' as the children repeated in hushed whispers) closely followed by Darth Maul, the Wicked Witch of the West, Cruella De Ville, Maleficent (the name of Snow White's wicked stepmother in the Disney film) and the Joker. At the time, neither Rebecca nor I had heard of Darth Maul and the boys took pleasure in explaining his role in *Star Wars* to us and correcting our spelling. We asked any members of the class who owned videos of stories to select from home sections where the villain appears and bring them into school for the next lesson. A letter was sent home explaining to the parents that this was part of the child's reading task. The following videos were brought in by children:

101 Dalmatians

Goldfinger

Sleeping Beauty

Snow White

Harry Potter and the Philosopher's Stone

Cartoon Capers

The Little Mermaid

Star Wars

The Wizard of Oz

Thomas the Tank Engine

The children had carefully wound their videos on at home to the appropriate moment when the 'baddie' comes into view. The class watched the selected clips, presented by each contributor, then after a repeat showing of each clip, followed by whole-class discussion, they were asked to analyse in detail the content of one episode of their choosing. We provided a pre-prepared grid as a guide. A group of three children's analysis of *101 Dalmatians* looked like this:

Film Title	Character	Appearance/ Dress	Face/ Expression/ Mood	Speech/ Tone	Actions
101 Dalmatians	Cruella de Ville	Very proud. Streaked hair black and white; black clothes. High heels.	Sneering face, bright red lips, curling lip. Scowls. Cunning smiles.	Scornful, mocks, shouts at staff, says 'fools', 'idiots'.	Clicks high heels, waves cigarette holder, smokes.

When the analysis of all the various film clips had been compiled they were used by the whole class to decide on the common characteristics of the evil characters involved. The children noted the use of strongly contrasted colours – red with black for example – or the dominance of a single shade, often black or white, which appeared to suggest both threat and power. They then commented on the powerful movements of the characters, such as striding, sweeping and swooping and also noted the cruelty of the voice tones employed. In this way they were beginning to uncover the patterns of meaning created through film language, both visual and auditory.

Analysing aspects of language use

As a way of looking more closely at the language used in books, the fifth column of the analysis grid, which recorded voice and tone, was used as the starting point for developing conversational exchanges, for confronting the villain and for 'hot seating' a particular villain, such as Voldemort and Cruella De Ville, to try to determine their motivation. They particularly enjoyed imitating the tones of voice employed in the films or inventing new ones to perform for one another. We then turned to a closer look at the language of the White Witch, the villain from

The Lion, the Witch and the Wardrobe. A close analysis of a section of this text highlighted what the children described as 'book language'. They thought this sounded 'slightly old-fashioned' but also 'very important'. They noted down the insults, commands and unanswerable questions (rhetorical ones) as being the main characteristics of the language of villains and they highlighted the following quotations on photocopies of the text:

'Speak vermin, or do you want my dwarf to get you a tongue with his whip?'
'Silence, fool!'
'Kill whoever you find there. You will know what to do.'
'Are you my counsellor or my slave? Do as you are told.'

They then completed a section in their own little books in which their main characters confronted the villain. Their language reflected their knowledge derived from these activities, as in the following words spoken by a skeleton from a boy's Spooky Land: 'Very well, I will go with you to that place, but be sure you cause me no trouble, human.' Another had his magician say:

'I'll show you my kingdom, scum, be afraid, be very, very afraid,' which blends a pattern of language echoed from the printed text with a famous film quotation.

One more, final activity was to produce a poem about their world based on Miroslav Holub's *Go and Open the Door* (1967) which begins:

Go and open the door
Maybe a dog's rummaging
Maybe you'll see a face, or an eye
or the picture of a picture

The children's poems, which were copied onto the back cover of their little books, all exhibited a fusion of the form of the stimulus poem with details of their own constructed fantasy worlds. This fusion can be seen in Emma's poem. It clearly echoes elements of the book and of her own imagined world (Figure 9.3).

Evaluating the writing process with the children

When the little books were completed (the project was conducted over a period of six weeks), the class engaged in a shared reading session where they exchanged their stories with each other. The readers were asked to identify the writer's specific, personal achievements. We then conducted a group evaluation of the whole project, asking the children first to note down individually what they had found helpful about the way we had organised the work. As a group we then negotiated how to record the evaluations. Our joint statements are reproduced below, giving first the comment agreed by the class, followed by an example (in italics) of individual children's actual comments. It is clear that the structures we had used had helped them to focus more confidently on the writing process.

Figure 9.3　Emma's poem

They had liked:

Breaking the work up so we did not have to write all in one go.
We didn't get bored with it.

Drawing the maps.
This helped us to think up good connecting place names.

Sharing our work by reading it out loud.
Made stories exciting – could do voices and act it out.

Watching each other's video clips.
Gave us good ideas for our own villains.

Feely bags were fun.
They helped us to describe what it would be like to walk in another world.

Writing in little books.
I felt like an author.

Using drawing alongside writing.
My drawings helped with descriptions and getting ideas.

Evaluating the whole project

Rebecca and I, in summarising our own evaluation, found that the children had been very motivated to write and genuinely interested in sharing each other's ideas, recognising the common currency of popular culture which allowed them to have their say. The emphasis on individual stories in the little books had freed them to discuss their own preoccupations outside the original fantasy framework (e.g. their chosen models for heroes were as diverse as Thomas the Tank Engine and James Bond). The planning activities we had devised had provided them with many opportunities for talk, while the Little Books had helped them to structure and sustain their work. We had provided extended activities with a particular focus on language choices which in turn had allowed reading and writing to support each other. All of this had been conducted within a planning framework attentive to the demands of external curricula, so that the fusion of teachers' and children's interests had been accomplished effectively.

A literacy of fusion

In reviewing the children's work at the end of the project, Rebecca and I concluded that the curriculum choices we had made had enabled us to establish a convergence of the demands made on her, working within a national framework for literacy, with the children's drives to establish their identities as individual writers among their peers. They had been eager to share their work and in their final, end-of-year assessment placed 'doing the little books' as their overall favourite activity despite the fact the work had been completed early in the school year.

The project had allowed them to work in a range of modalities, including visiting websites to consult for information about some of the villains. Moreover, one of the major modalities, that of talk, had been central to the processes of planning and sharing. The class had enjoyed many opportunities to contribute to group discussion and to read or perform their work. The planning devices, usually very simple sheets which allowed them to draw up ideas for characters or settings in words or pictures, had made the structuration of narrative and the possibilities of narrative choice visible to the children and allowed those with more visual imaginations to record their ideas more easily. Word and sentence level work, so central to current structures in England's Literacy Strategy, was embedded in the shared reading and writing and not presented on worksheets as isolated activities. The work had also enabled us to begin to introduce more complex media skills such as the analysis of the visual semiotic clues, provided in the videos by clothes and mannerisms as well as actions and speeches. The class was well on the way to understanding how to conduct a content analysis, a skill often reserved for the secondary phase of schooling. Not only this, but in sharing the children's worlds Rebecca and I had gained a more complex understanding of their cultural interests and shared pleasures.

The reading, drawing, viewing, oral telling and writing had become intertwined so that every child was enabled to work from a perceived strength and no one child's personal knowledge was rejected by the group. A good example of this is the boy whose piece, 'Monster Argument', is given above. He gained real confidence from his ability to mimic speech and direct his group in performing this and other little scenarios, rather like Dyson's (1997) account of the use of author theatre in *Writing Superheroes*. It was also true of another boy's use of a 'Thomas the Tank' narrative which the others listened to with interest, rather than giving a blanket rejection of its inappropriate 'babyishness'. Similarly, Rebecca was led to question her own immediate knee-jerk rejection of the James Bond story's lack of relevance, when the boy who had chosen it as his source of villains gave a complex account of how an opponent could be defeated without violence, taking his information from the Bond film text. Her instinct not to allow what she deemed to be too adult material into her classroom had been motivated by all the reasons researchers report that teachers often give for rejecting the use of popular culture (Dyson 1997; Green *et al.* 1998; Lambirth 2003; Makin & Jones Diaz 2002; Marsh & Millard 2003). It was interesting to see how much this child gained from acceptance of his current obsessive interest and how he chose to select relevant aspects of the spy narrative to fit the fantasy work of the classroom. Perhaps we underestimate children's own understanding of what is appropriate in different contexts too readily and do not allow sufficient scope for this form of transformation.

Developing professional confidence

Marsh (2003) has conducted research into the 'self-sanctioning' behaviour of trainee teachers, which prevents them from incorporating aspects of children's culture which they nevertheless acknowledge as having the power to motivate. She attributes the mismatch between their reported beliefs and practices partly to the operation of the strong framing of the curriculum which takes the control of much of the content, organisation and delivery of what is to be taught away from the teacher or pupil.

The strategies of a literacy framework based on shared reading and writing had, however, served us well, promoting the discussion and sharing of key elements of the fantasy genre on a macro level and niceties of composition and style on the micro level. The difference in the boldness of curriculum conception as developed by Rebecca as class teacher and the hesitancy of Lambirth's teachers who thought that popular culture had no place in school (2003) is one of professional confidence. Rebecca's individual conclusions were summed up in the following comment recorded at the time of review:

> The children are so involved . . . the fact that it stretches their imagination and their verbal interaction with each other. That way that I could make it cross boundaries, so you could start with literature and, OK, from your literature point of view you're getting written work and poetry and you can expand into, say, newspaper articles and get other activities out of it. In this case we looked at snow and snowflakes for our science work.

Conclusion

If fantasy is the currency of the unofficial curriculum, brought into school most readily by the children themselves, reading and writing still remain keystones for access to the official curriculum and it is with the latter that teachers wish to engage most directly. Rebecca's key role as teacher lay in her ability to fuse important aspects of the children's understanding of how fantasy narratives work, which they had derived from their implicit understanding of more visual texts, with the rich literary language of a well-loved children's classic. This ability to fuse the preoccupations of home and school and to motivate children to experiment with the languages of media other than that of the printed text is an essential element of the fusion literacy concept I have sought to promote (Millard 2003a). It requires teachers to be attentive to children's interests and preferred ways of creating meaning, in order to enable them to both question and transform knowledge brought from their interests outside to meet the needs of the classroom. As Marsh (2003) concludes, it is the 'message' to teachers that there is no necessary prohibition on the use of other media in the primary classroom, that is most crucial at a time of strong curriculum framing. There is a professional responsibility for educationalists to support teachers to contribute to the construction of their own autonomous literacy curricula to match the needs and interests of their classes while yet addressing imperatives from national directives.

Implications for practice

The concerns of this chapter have been to illustrate how children's and teachers' purposes can support rather than work against one another. The first requirement is for teachers to be allowed the autonomy to decide what is appropriate in the context of their own teaching and learning context. This requires active support from educationalists through collaborative workshops and seminars which enable teachers to gain the professional confidence to take risks and share the insights gained from their experimentation with new forms. Teachers should have the confidence to:

- **Take an interest in children's out-of-school literacy practices through regular discussions in class**

Make a habit of surveying the interests of a new class using simple questions about the kinds of reading and writing they do at home. Include screen-based and computer activities in this survey.

- **Look for opportunities to allow all class members to contribute what they already know about storytelling**

Let them talk about the films and videos that they watch and the computer games they play as well as the books they read. Trust the children to find ways of transforming their current knowledge to appropriate forms in their school work.

- **Allow children to benefit from being experts about aspects of popular culture**

Give them opportunities to explain their ideas and interests to others. Foster a tolerance of others' tastes and views through open discussion.

- **Structure writing activities which encourage collaborative work and enable the kind of talk that allows children to retell their own stories to each other**

Build on the narratives they have encountered in other media and encourage them to employ the modes of meaning-making they find most productive.

- **Emphasise the importance of being critical about the texts children both read and write**

For example, find opportunities to help them to discuss issues of racial and gender stereotyping, commercialism, and the differences that they encounter between print and filmic versions of a particular story.

- Tolerate differences in taste and in individuals' preferred modes of creativity

Pay as much attention to aspects of design and the visual impact of a text as to its language content. Enable children to draw on their preferred modes in planning and presenting their work to others and in this manner encourage a sense of audience and purpose for writing.

- Involve parents and carers as much as possible

Consider sending work home. Set tasks that include reading visual as well as more conventional stories.

References

Appleyard, J.A. & S.J (1990) *Becoming a Reader: The Experience of Fiction From Childhood to Adulthood.* New York: Cambridge University Press.

Bettleheim, B. & Zelan, K. (1982) *On Learning to Read: A Child's Fascination With Meaning.* London: Thames and Hudson.

Blume, J. (2001) *Forever.* London: Macmillan's Children's Books (First published 1975).

Bourdieu, P. (1984) *Distinction: A Social Critique of the Judgement of Taste.* London: Routledge and Kegan Paul.

Bruner, J. (1999) *The Culture of Education* (Fifth edition). Cambridge, MA: Harvard University Press.

Burgess, M. (1996) *Junk.* London: Pelican Books.

Byatt, A.S. (2004) 'Happily Ever After', *Guardian Review*, 4 January.

Cox, B. (ed.) (1998) *Literacy Is Not Enough: Essays on the Importance of Reading.* Manchester: Manchester University Press.

Dreamworks (2001) *Shrek.* Home Entertainment VHS Tape.

Dyson, A.H. (1997) *Writing Superheroes: Contemporary Childhood, Popular Culture, and Classroom Literacy.* New York: Teachers College Press.

Dyson, A.H. (2000) 'On Reframing Children's Words: The Perils, Promises and Pleasures of Writing Children', *Research in the Teaching of English*, 34, 352–67.

Dyson, A.H. (2003) *Brothers and Sisters Learn to Write: Popular Literacies in Childhood and School Cultures.* New York: Teachers College Press.

Gilbert, P. (1992) 'Narrative as gendered social practice: in search of different story lines for language research', *Linguistics and Education*, 5, 211–18.

Green, B., Reid, J. & Bigum, C. (1998) 'Teaching the Nintendo generation? Children, computer culture and popular technologies', in S. Howard (ed.) *Wired-up: Young People and the Electronic Media.* London: UCL Press.

Heath, S.B. (1983) *Ways With Words: Language, Life and Work in Communities and Classrooms.* Cambridge: Cambridge University Press.

Hilton, M. (ed.) (1996) *Potent Fictions: Children's Literacy and the Challenge of Popular Culture.* London: Routledge.

Holub, M. (1969) *Collected Poems*, Modern European Poets. Harmondsworth: Penguin.

Lambirth, A. (2003) ' "They get enough of that at home" understanding aversion to popular culture in schools', *Reading, Literacy and Language*, 37(1), 9–14.

Lankshear, C. with Gee, J.P., Knobel, M. & Searle, C. (1997) *Changing Literacies*. Buckingham: Open University Press.

Lewis, C.S. (2001) *The Lion, the Witch and the Wardrobe (Chronicles of Narnia)*. London: Collins (First published 1950).

Makin, L. & Jones Diaz, C. (2002) *Literacies in Early Childhood: Changing Views and Challenging Practice*. Sydney: Maclennan and Petty.

Marsh, J. (2003) 'Taboos, Tightropes and Trivial Pursuits: Pre-service and Newly-qualified Teachers' Beliefs and Practices in Relation to Popular Culture and Literacy'. Paper presented at AERA Annual Meeting, Chicago, April 2003.

Marsh, J. (2004) 'The techno-literacy practices of young children', *Journal of Early Childhood Research*, 2(1), 51–66.

Marsh, J. & Millard, E. (2000) *Literacy and Popular Culture: Using Children's Culture in the Classroom*. London: Paul Chapman.

Marsh, J. & Millard, E. (2003) *Literacy and Popular Culture in the Classroom*. Reading: National Centre for Language and Literacy, The University of Reading.

Millard E. (2003a) 'Transformative Pedagogy: Towards a Literacy of Fusion', *Reading, Literacy and Language*, 37(1), 3–9.

Millard, E. (2003b) 'Transformative Practitioners, Transformative Practice: Teachers Working with Popular Culture in the Classroom'. Paper presented at AERA Annual Meeting, Chicago, April 2003.

Millard, E. (in press). 'To Enter the Castle of Fear: Engendering Children's Story Writing from Home to School at KS 2', *Gender in Education*.

Moss, E. (1977) 'The peppermint lesson', in M. Meek, A. Warlow & G. Barton (eds) *The Cool Web*. London: Bodley Head.

Pennac, D. (1994) *Reads Like a Novel*. London: Quartet Books.

Seiter, E. (1999) 'Power Rangers at Preschool: Negotiating Media in Child Care Settings', in M. Kinder (ed.) (1999) *Kids' Media Culture*. Durham: Duke University Press.

Spufford, F. (2002) *The Child That Books Built: A Life in Reading*. London: Faber and Faber.

Tatar, M. (ed.) (2004) *The Annotated Brothers Grimm: Jacob Grimm, Wilhelm Grimm*. New York, London: WW Norton.

Tolkien, J.R.R. (1991) *The Hobbit*. London: HarperCollins (First published 1937).

Wells, G. (1987) *The Meaning Makers: Children Learning Language and Using Language to Learn*. London: Hodder & Stoughton.

Wells, G. (2003) 'Action, talk and text: integrating literacy with other modes of meaning making', in E. Bearne, H. Dombey, and T. Grainger, (eds) *Classroom Interactions in Literacy*, Maidenhead: McGrawHill Educational, Open University Press.

Wilkinson, K. (2003) 'Children's favourite books', *Early Childhood Literacy*, 3(3), 1.

CHAPTER 10

Getting it right for children
Making meaningful connections between culture, community and school

Dominic Scott

For today's children, a new childhood beckons. The traditional educators – family, church and school – no longer hold the monopoly on how children learn. They need to become literate in areas such as computers, pop culture, fashion and technological gadgetry with new levels of sophistication that often make them 'smarter' than their parents. Nowhere is this more urgent than among immigrant children. This chapter illustrates how committed teenagers (govies) enabled nine- and ten-year-old children of migrant workers to critically read their new world. It urges educators to broaden their definition of literacy and to embrace innovative strategies which incorporate critical approaches that help children understand the new texts that are meaningful to their lives. It also shows how the school curriculum can be made more meaningful for children if their cultural capital is taken into consideration.

Introduction

Children today live in a world of unimagined complexity. The 'new childhood' is a social construction that transcends parents, schools and civic society. Many factors contribute to this construction: corporations, media, the Internet, toys, video games, peers and popular culture. All create spaces within which children read and interpret the world and its expectations of them, and within which they create images of themselves. These myriad sources of knowledge and information offer interpretations of reality beyond those offered by traditional institutions such as the family, church and school; and help initiate children to become competent in a world of hyperreality. By hyperreality I mean spaces in which simulations are accepted as real, and the distinction between media-generated images and real-world images is blurred and permeable. This represents a new form of construction in which mainstream culture is eclipsed by media- and corporate-generated culture.

Knowledge of and access to these hyperrealities creates a sense of power in children as they learn to negotiate the postmodern world. This has resulted in a new awareness of power in which 'children's access to the adult world via the electronic media of hyperreality has subverted contemporary children's consciousness of themselves as incompetent and dependent entities' (Steinberg & Kincheloe 1998: 17). The very distinction between childhood and adulthood has become permeable, as children outsmart and upstage adults in their knowledge of popular culture, technology and market-generated consumption.

Text, no longer exclusively represented by the written word, must now include a panoply of artefacts including video games, television, music and toys, all of which coalesce to form an almost seamless world of knowledge, meaning, feelings and beliefs within which the modern child dwells. These, in turn, are moulded to conform to the desires of marketers, corporations, governments and civic agencies, all of whom have helped create them. To be 'literate', the modern child is required to acquire multiple literacies in many codes and formats. This presents additional challenges for children who must distinguish meaning and significance in the multiplicity of codifications constructed by others. Put another way, children have to decide which hyperreality is the relevant and meaningful one amid an array of competing hyperrealities. To be literate, the postmodern child must feel powerful in several different contexts, each with very different literacies.

Children learn that there are multiple literacies required for multiple realities, and that the codes of one may not apply within the context of the other. Competency in multiple literacies thus becomes the essential skill for successful negotiation of the new childhood. Within this deluge of information, the modern child is confronted with the challenge of making meaning of the world and its competing realities. Thus the nature of childhood is transformed in ways whereby 'children, adults, parents, and childhood professionals are caught in a zeitgeist of cultural transition in the meaning of childhood' (Kincheloe 2002: 109). Children have to make meaning of the world, and require knowledgeable others who will act as mediators (Vygotsky 1962). However, in the postmodern world, parents and other adults are often not available to act as mediators. Furthermore, adults often have little comprehension of the realities of the cultural neighbourhood that children inhabit. Consequently, the media and other forms of digital interfaces act as surrogate mediators for children. Vygotsky (1962) recognised the complex cultural embeddedness of human psychological processes:

> A basic tenet of Vygotsky's approach to psychology is that human behaviour is too complex to isolate, dissect, and study in a vacuum. It must instead be studied in the social and historical context within which it occurs. Thus this approach is *sociohistorical*.
>
> (Dixon-Krauss 1996: 1)

What Vygotsky (1962) and others saw as signifiers – words and phrases that acted as tools for the development of abstract thought and concept formation – have been radically augmented to a large extent by digitalised signifiers that are more concentrated and more powerful than any previously anticipated. We only have to think how naturally a seven-year-old grasps instant text messaging or emoticons to understand the sophistication of our digitally mediated cultural tools. This new comprehension marks a dramatic evolution of signification, a compression of concepts within a single mediational tool such as a word or phrase. (Guy Merchant's chapter in this book shows us wonderful examples of children's abilities in this area.)

From the above it is clear that literacy must be defined in a broader context than the familiar dictionary definition: 'the condition or quality of being literate, especially the ability to read and write' (Morris 1977: 762). Increasingly, literacy involves competency in a variety of media, of which reading and writing are but a part. Nevertheless, they remain a central part, since the written word is still the privileged medium of expression in a knowledge-based society. Competency in the world still requires the ability to read and write. However, this competency goes beyond the mere technical skills of sentence construction and essay writing, and embraces the ability to speak in multiple literacies to multiple realities. Much of the acquisition of these literacies happens by osmosis in spaces inhabited by children, but constructed by corporations, media and digitally generated interfaces.

The power relations of literacy

One of the great conundrums of this new alignment of childhood access to powerful mediative tools is the issue of falling scores in reading in the US: 'Compared to 2000, a few more states reported positive results [in reading] for 2001 in eighth grade. But scores fell in grades 4, 5 and 10, extending declines already in place' (Loveless 2002: 4). The contrast between cyber-savvy children and falling literacy rates has been cited by various authors. Patrick Finn (1999) asserted, 'As working-class children progress through school, their reading scores fall further and further below their actual grade level. We presume they don't have the basics, and we give them more phonics' (Finn 1999: 90). What could account for the falling reading scores of working-class children despite their growing competence in computer literacy? In his study of working-class youth in English schools, Willis (1977) portrayed the school as a site for the formalised exchange of high-status knowledge for co-operation. This high-status knowledge is the language of success in middle- and upper-class society. In order to have the necessary literacy for success, children willingly give co-operation to their teachers. Willis referred to this as the *basic teaching paradigm*:

> This idea concerns teaching as a fair exchange – most basically of knowledge for respect, of guidance for control. Since knowledge is the rarer commodity this gives the teacher his moral superiority. This is the dominant educational paradigm which

stands outside particular teachers but enables them to exert control legitimately upon the children.

(Willis 1977: 64)

The majority of children accepted this deal because they perceived formal education as the key to economic success, social status and personal efficacy. However, some children did not co-operate in this bargain. They perceived the language of success as a cultural sell-out and selectively identifed with, and even glorified, working-class values. The irony was that, rather than becoming liberated through class identity, these youth became doomed to low-paid and low-status jobs. It is also ironic that the factory jobs, which provided the economic basis for working-class pride, largely disappeared overseas with free trade and globalisation.

Ogbu (1991) studied the different perspectives of recent immigrant minority children (voluntary minorities) and American-born minority children (involuntary minorities). He argued that immigrant minorities saw themselves as here by choice, with the option of returning home. Further, they saw their tribulations as stepping-stones to a better life. Knowing where they came from, and conscious of the support they would have upon returning, they engaged in *accommodation* to their new culture rather than *assimilation* into it. By contrast the American-born minorities perceived themselves as cut off from the nourishment of their native cultures and marooned in the dominant culture. Consequently, they acquired a caste-like status, seeing themselves as permanently oppressed. For them, the good life as defined by mainstream society was unobtainable, and thus they had to glorify their own culture.

Lisa Delpit (1995) addressed this reaction to the subordination of involuntary minorities to mainstream aspirations. She realised that:

> literacy is much more than reading and writing, but rather that it is part of a larger political entity. This larger entity he [James Paul Gee] calls a discourse, construed as something of an 'identity kit' . . . examples of which might be the discourse of lawyers, the discourse of academics, or the discourse of men.

(Delpit 1995: 153)

She outlined the idea of the importance of discourses in determining attitudes and social acceptance. For her, *primary* discourses are ways of communication that one grows up with, while *secondary* discourses are those one acquires or buys into for social, economic or professional reasons. She suggests that acquisition of higher status discourses by involuntary minorities is particularly difficult and fraught with the likelihood of cultural disintegration and loss of identity. However, successful voluntary immigrants quickly adopt these secondary discourses, particularly those associated with success-orientated groups, as a way of quickly advancing to higher status positions. They see no contradiction in code-shifting to suit the occasion, nor do they see it as a cultural sell-out. Rather, they perceive it as the 'cost of doing business'. It does not involve any compromise of who they perceive themselves to be, nor do they feel colonised by the experience. Involuntary minorities on the other hand see any adoption of the discourse of higher status groups as a cultural disaster.

Delpit (1995) railed against the notion that American-born, involuntary minorities cannot or should not acquire high-status discourses, and advocated that they are especially in need of this language of success. She believed that minority children can be taught 'the rules for dominant discourses, allowing students to succeed in mainstream America who were not only born outside of the realms of power and status, but who had no access to status institutions' (p.159). She also asserted that it is the teacher's responsibility to overcome student resistance to school discourse, to move them beyond the notion that to be successful in school is to 'become white'. She believed that it is most desirable for involuntary minorities to don the discourse of success without feeling diminished in the process.

What Delpit (1995) is referring to here is a change of consciousness, one that is brought about through endless effort by the teacher. Student liberation can best be facilitated, not by singing the praises of their primary discourses, but by teaching them the multiple literacies necessary for success in mainstream society, and by fostering the belief that dominant discourses can be used to transform main-stream society. Rather than fear the loss of identity associated with the dominant discourse, teachers should inculcate the belief that fluency in the mainstream discourse is essential to transform it.

The idea of becoming a creator of language rather than merely a consumer of it has been expounded by Paulo Freire (1997). In his work with adult illiterates in Brazil in the 1960s, Freire attempted to move his students from a 'banking' system of learning to a dynamic, creative process which he called 'critical literacy': 'From the beginning, we rejected the hypothesis of a purely mechanistic literacy program and considered the problem of teaching adults how to read in relation to the awakening of their consciousness' (Freire 1994: 43). At that time in Brazil (1964), 'approximately four million school-age children lacked school' (p. 41).

Freire created cultural circles where community leaders worked with adult illiter-ates to debate issues that were important to them. The circle identified *generative* words that embodied deep meaning for the learners. These are words from the life of the community, its experiences, hopes and realities. Since they were the learners' own words, they were very much at home with them, and were deeply embedded in their emotional and economic realities. They became aware that they had *expertise* in the area that the words represented. Their understanding of the meaning of these words was intrinsic and genuine. They could talk authentically about the topics these words represented. It was around these generative words that Freire and his workers created the literacy curriculum. Generative words became the supercharged symbols of the students' realities, and hence became important words that they were motivated to debate, spell and write. It is clear that Freire's approach is built on learner-created artefacts, words and themes, as opposed to pre-selected topics in commercial books and primers: 'The important thing . . . is for the people to come to feel like masters of their thinking by discussing the thinking and views of the world explicitly or implicitly manifest in their own suggestions' (Freire 1997: 105).

Finn (1999), Ogbu (1991), Delpit (1995) and Freire (1997) each perceived the deeper power structure of literacy. For them, literacy involved acquiring the ability to take part in the discourses of power and the powerful. Rather than teach functional literacy, these authors believed that critical literacy, the ability to talk and relate powerfully in ways that helped shape one's own destiny, was a much more effective motivator for learners to acquire the multiple literacies of post-modernism. How then do these theories relate to children, particularly children who are on the margins of society and are denied access to the power literacies of US society? An opportunity to put some of these ideas into practice came about when a group of migrant children was able to take part in a summer workshop that focused on critical literacy for migrant children.

The Migrant Literacy Project

Each year the Federally funded Migrant Education Program at Millersville University, Pennsylvania, provides a summer school experience for school children aged four to 17 years. The rich farming county in which Millersville is located has a tradition of employing migrant workers seasonally on local farms. Frequently, whole families accompany and help their parents with the work. In addition, migrant families often settle in the area, yet continue to experience frequent relocations because of economic difficulties and job changes. Any child who has recently moved and whose parents work in an agriculture-based job can qualify for Migrant Education services. These children often receive inadequate education and tend to experience regression during the summer months. To compensate for these factors, the Migrant Education Program provides a summer programme for the children at a local high school to help them maintain their English language skills. The children served by the Migrant Education Program are almost exclusively Hispanic, the majority of whom are of Puerto Rican descent. However, not all of the children are immigrants. Many of these minority children speak Spanish as their primary language and are at various stages of English language acquisition.

In the summer of 2003 a unique partnership was developed between the Migrant Education Program and the Pennsylvania Governor's School for Teaching. The Governor's School consisted of a five-week residential experience for outstanding junior level (16- and 17-year-old) high school students from across Pennsylvania who wanted to become teachers. To make their teaching experience more authentic it was decided to orient the Governor's School towards a more authentic involvement in teaching migrant children from a critical perspective. The school's director felt that if the 16- and 17-year-old participants (commonly referred to as 'govies') were to be properly prepared for the real world of teaching in an increasingly diverse society, they should be exposed to populations of children who are representative of these diversities. The Migrant Education Program organisers agreed to this partnership with the school and as a result 64 govies spent two weeks helping five- to 11-year-old migrant education children to develop literacy skills from a critical perspective.

Governor's School preparation for critical literacy

The govies were given an introduction to the teaching of migrant children from a critical perspective. This consisted of a four-part programme with experts in different aspects of critical literacy.

1   The first part consisted of a workshop with the Migrant Education Program director that outlined strategies for adjusting lesson plans for children who were English language learners. It emphasised acceptance of children for what they are, the necessity of seeing the children's culture as a strength, and the importance of co-operative learning strategies and the language experience approach.

2   A one-hour seminar was arranged with Marta Benevides, an international consultant in literacy from El Salvador who is currently working with the United Nations. Marta drew the connection between literacy and empowerment. She emphasised the place of immigrants in the provision of basic necessities of life for Western consumers, particularly farm workers and meat processing plant operators. Marta emphasised how education and liberation promoted the ideals of a culture of peace in the world.

3   The Governor's School Director spoke to the govies about the growing diversity of the American student population, and the need to understand and incorporate the children's cultures and strengths into lesson planning.

4   The govies took part in a multicultural awareness game called 'Bá Fá Bá Fá'. This simulation game required them to break into two groups and rehearse the language and practices of their make-believe cultural group (the Alphans or the Betans). Each group was allowed to send visitors to the other group and report back in an attempt to understand the 'others'. A debriefing of the whole group allowed participants to see how they had misinterpreted, became impatient with, or devalued the other group. This game provided the govies with first-hand experience of what it feels like to be an outsider, unable to understand how a different culture works. It also let them see the type of resiliency and resource-fulness necessary to acquire the language of success of another culture. In a debriefing session afterwards the govies began to think about how they would try to apply these insights to their teaching with the migrant children.

Following their initial training, the govies were required to teach in groups of three, and to take responsibility for the course content in one of six subject areas: maths, science, English, social studies, art and music. The classes all had a certified teacher and a teacher's assistant present, but the govies were to take responsibility for a half-day of instruction for two weeks, organised around a unifying theme that promoted critical literacy. The climax of the experience was a trip to the Hans Herr House, a local farm museum showcasing the Mennonite lifestyle in Pennsylvania. It was felt that this culminating experience would provide a focal point for the lessons as well as illustrate for the children the diverse tradition of the area and the struggles of immigrant groups over the centuries to succeed in a new country.

In order to focus on the children's experiences more fully, three govies, each from different ethnic backgrounds, were asked to keep journals over the period of their two-week teaching assignment. Ryan was an Irish-American male, while Neha and Payal were both bilingual females from India. The team of three worked with a class of 25 nine- and ten-year-old children of migrant agricultural workers.

The children's work with the govies

In their journals the govies were asked to respond to the following questions:

- What information or skills were you trying to impart to your children?
- How did you use the children's own generic words to engage them?
- How were your lessons culturally relevant?
- What have you done to become familiar with the children's cultures?
- How did you know they became engaged in the lessons?

A mentor assisted the govies with lesson planning, classroom observations and debriefing. Ryan, Neha and Payal were assigned to a science class, but it was made clear that in all subject areas the basic reading and writing skills necessary to become effective communicators in English were to be focused on. Of key importance here was the belief that the govies would implement critical literacy practices as advocated in their preparation seminars, rather than revert back to the 'basic teaching paradigm' as outlined by Willis (1977).

The three govies in the team reflected on their assignment and the preconceptions they brought to the task. Neha recalled, 'When I think of migrant education I think of chaos. I picture a bunch of children being unco-operative, loud and extremely active. I really hope the children will listen to us and at least give us a chance.' This admission helped her to draw upon her own cultural strengths and resiliency: 'I am not really worried about the language barrier in migrant education. Being a minority and helping my mother with her English has made me patient and under-standing towards people learning a new language.' She was already seeing literacy acquisition as a transformative, liberating experience. Ryan's first exposure to the class was very positive: 'Our time at the migrant program was wonderful. There were 17 of them from Vietnam (Binh), the Dominican Republic, Peru, Puerto Rico and several other places. They had been in the US between four months and eight years.' Payal expressed some reticence:

> Today is our first day at the Migrant Education Program. I'm a little nervous and not sure what to expect. I think this will be a great experience for us all. I expect to learn a lot, but even if I don't come away making an impact, I hope to be happy with my work here.

The children were excited to see the govies and accepted them with enthusiasm.

The first lesson the team chose to teach was on classification. They felt that this was an essential concept for both science and English, and a useful way into creating a consciousness of how people are also 'sorted' in society. The team collected a variety of candies of different shapes, colours, textures and types, and put a variety on each table. No explanation was offered initially. The children were asked to define the word 'classification'. Several children expressed a clear understanding of the concept: one ventured 'separating stuff' while another said 'using it in science'. The team wrote a formal definition of 'classification' on the board and asked the children how they might classify the candies. One child said, 'hard candies and soft candies', after which they were paired and asked to classify the candies using the method they had selected.

When the task was complete, the children were asked to share their classification systems. Several children shared their choices: hard/soft, small/large, long/square, triangles/circles. When asked, 'What problems did you come across?' the children reported that not all candies fell into their pre-selected categories, for example, not all candies were hard or soft. The team then asked the children how they would apply classification in real life. Specifically they asked, 'How would you classify people?' They offered 'skin colour', 'size', 'male/female', 'ugly/pretty', 'language', 'workers/not workers', 'rich/poor' and 'hair colour' as possible categorisation criteria. It seemed clear that children were beginning to reveal their generative words that Paulo Freire identified in his work with illiterate Brazilian peasants. The children were learning to 'decodify' their world and thereby graft literacy acquisition (reading the word) with an understanding of their environment (reading the world).

At the same time that Freire was working in Brazil, Sylvia Ashton Warner was making similar discoveries about children's literacy acquisition in her work with Maori children in New Zealand. She realised that there were significant words for children that carried powerful meaning for them:

> Writing must be cohesive. An integrated, developing idea. Every word present must be part of a grand design. A necessary part. Every morning after a period of free conversation, my Little Ones, right down to the fives, write of something close to them. The words they use are words of *their* choosing, and are necessary to them and are part of the developing idea in their young minds. There is a sequence in what they write, an intense meaning, since each child writes about that thing that is on his mind.
>
> (Ashton-Warner 1971: 176)

Note the close relationship between Freire's *generative words* and Ashton-Warner's *intense meaning* embodied in the children's words. Ashton-Warner went on to state, 'education, fundamentally, is the increase of the percentage of the conscious in relation to the unconscious' (p.176). Freire (1997) described this as 'conscientization', a process by which '. . . the people come to feel like masters of their thinking by discussing the thinking and the views of the world explicitly or implicitly manifest in their own suggestions and those of their comrades' (p.105).

In the second lesson the govies started by reviewing the previous day's work. Neha identified the reasons for doing so:

> We decided to review the classification lesson from yesterday. We want to record the children's ideas because they were *creative* and we want to acknowledge that. We are going to display a poster of the children's ideas so they can always look at it and realise that they were *creators* of a classification system.

She was clearly aware of the empowering aspect of education, and the need for educators to emphasise student achievement and progress in their abilities to construct their own learning.

This second lesson centred on getting the children prepared for their field trip to Hans Herr House Museum. The visit would include hands-on activities which the children would be expected to do. One of these activities involved manipulating flax and learning how this crop had, in previous centuries, been used to make cloth in Pennsylvania. Neha again reported in her journal, 'This lesson is culturally relevant because it is about land and how something is grown in a specific atmosphere.' The lesson began by asking the children if they knew what flax was. One child said it was a plant. One of the govies produced two posters that illustrated how flax was grown, harvested and eventually processed into linen. The children were asked to identify the qualities of seeds. This was an attempt to connect this lesson with the previous one on classification. The children suggested several aspects of seeds (hard, soft, large, small) that may be used in a classification system. The children were then asked to pretend that they were a flax seed and were asked how that feels. The children were given a response sheet asking them to describe their feelings as a flax seed as they go from being a seed to becoming a shirt. As a follow-up, the children were asked to draw a scene from their story. Payal noted in her journal that:

> The children differed with their responses to the writing. Some were enthusiastic while others were unsure of what was going on. Some kids wanted to write in Spanish. I could tell that most children were engaged in the lesson through their questions. Some asked questions about flax, while others wanted to make sure they were completing the task properly. I think the children were successful because all of them had at least two sentences down on their paper. Some of them had filled up all of the lines on their paper.

When the children had finished, they were asked if anyone would like to share their story and two children volunteered. In her journal Neha commented, 'I was really surprised to see Manuel volunteer to share first. I have never seen him volunteer for anything. I was really proud of him.' Perhaps Manuel's enthusiasm was a result of being given the opportunity to express his feelings and hence the emotions that are important to him.

The third lesson built on the previous two. The govies wanted to introduce the concept of land forms and they felt that the children could relate to land forms with which they were familiar. Here, the govies began to experience some difficulties and it was Ryan who recorded his frustration:

> My lesson was a disaster. It started well enough but from there, things just went downhill . . . It was suggested that I personally plan a lesson conforming to my opinion of what children could handle. I thought that rivers were a perfect subject, as many of them [the children] once lived in places where water would be a threat, and if they went to the South and worked there someday it could be very useful knowledge.

Ryan was trying to be a dialogical, problem-posing teacher by presenting information in an 'organized, systematized, and developed "re-presentation" to individuals of the things about which they want to know more' (Freire 1997: 74). Ryan felt it was his place to define what 'useful knowledge' was, but he appeared to have repeated the mistake wherein 'many political and educational plans have failed because their authors designed them according to their own personal views of reality' (Freire 1997: 75). This was a humbling experience for the govies, and a valuable lesson in creating the balance of teacher-prepared lessons and student-created generative words and themes. Despite this, Ryan continued to see it as a classroom management issue: 'Next time, I would set up a solid discipline system so that I could teach.' His view was not shared by the others and it was Neha who identified the source of the failure:

> I don't think the lesson was successful at all. The concepts were too in-depth. The kids weren't listening because there really weren't many visual aids for them to be excited about. Many of the kids had no idea of what was going on. I really think things need to be done simpler and slower. The kids were consistent when it came to their interests. They were excited and paid attention when the actual hands-on experiment started. But when it was over everything was chaotic again.

The govies struggled to make the content relevant to the children in many ways. What was important was the dialogue and search for meaning in the responses of the children. As the govies pondered the children's engagement with the class activities, they formed opinions of the significance of their efforts. Neha felt that she had gained significant insights into critical approaches to literacy:

> I feel that in many cases I learnt more from the children through their discussions of personal experiences. I've learnt that there really is a connection between the children's culture and the way they react to certain situations. Culturally appropriate teaching is extremely difficult for me, but I've realised it is extremely important to relate lessons to cultures because that's the only way to learn the importance of the lesson. When children understand what they learn by relating it to their own culture, they will never forget it.

This type of realisation underscores the power of critical literacy and the need to engage children in the lessons in a meaningful way. The experiences of Ryan, Neha and Payal illustrate the potential of short induction programmes and continuing dialogue in preparing new teachers for critical practices in teaching literacy to young children.

Conclusions

These three lessons illustrate the possibilities and pitfalls of attempting critical literacy in the classroom. On the one hand the govies saw the potential of relating their curriculum to the children's lives and experiences. However, even after some success with getting the children to offer their own generative words, there was a tendency to fall back upon teacher-selected themes and concerns. The road to creating a curriculum based on children's *generative words* or *intense meanings* requires educators who are confident of their assumptions and committed to student empowerment above teacher direction. The commitment to a child-empowering classroom requires courage, resourcefulness and trust that only comes with time. Lack of experience, pressures and insecurity work against the poise and resiliency necessary to let go of controlling the class and allowing the children to generate the themes and literacies they consider important and relevant. The fear of imminent chaos is always present. Unfortunately, the 'default setting' of many educators in a climate of accountability tends to be teacher-centred and teacher-directed.

This chapter began with the assertion that children today are required to become literate in many contexts, and that technology, media, computer games and toys grant them unprecedented access to competencies that go beyond the promise of school reading programmes. The concept of 'text' has taken on a new meaning, one that requires efficacy in a variety of worlds and realities. Schools and educators must position themselves at the centre of this new childhood or be seen as irrelevant to the great literacy project of our time. Children feel an affinity with efficacy in multiple worlds and expect schools to help them enfold their many realities into a meaningful skein of competencies. A quantum shift towards literacy as a multifaceted construct moulded by children in response to multiple realities is required. This is not the same thing as the teacher stepping aside and letting chaos reign. It does, however, require that teachers believe that children create their own learning and that they actively make meaning of many worlds simultaneously. By repositioning classrooms at the centre of their meaning-making and allowing children to generate a large element of the classroom themes and discourse, teachers can empower children to meaningfully weave the many literacies they experience into the fabric of their lives. Some suggestions as to how teachers might go about this work are outlined below.

Implications for practice

- **See literacy as multifaceted**

Finn (1999) identifies four types of literacy: performative, functional, informative and powerful literacy. Ask yourself, 'What type of literacy am I asking my children to exhibit?' If your answer is mostly performative and functional, consider that children often pick up these skills in the pursuit of informational and powerful literacy. Do your children get the opportunity to evaluate critique, and to analyse events, ideas and beliefs? Their worlds are full of opportunities for discussion of critical questions. Assume you are a visitor from outer space. Ask questions about their lives, current affairs, popular trends and artefacts, and ask children to explain why things are as they are.

- ## Acknowledge that children critically evaluate their worlds

Children scan the multiplicity of data, information and knowledge offered to them and select those items they consider to be relevant to their lives. Is your teaching relevant to their needs? Consider linking every new idea, skill or concept to a known attention-getter for your children. Knowledge of the children's cultural background, economic conditions and lived worlds will be important in generating these connections. By embedding lessons within a critical analysis of their worlds, teachers can help children distil what is important for them while seeing classroom lessons as relevant to their quest for meaning-making.

- ## Work at creating a dialogical classroom

You can do this by removing your own concepts of teacher-learner hierarchy and experiment with the teacher-as-learner model. It is not a question of 'who has the most knowledge?' but rather 'there can only be trust between us when I acknowledge that I have something to learn from you.' This is sometimes referred to as creating a respectful classroom. Children who know that their knowing is honestly solicited by a teacher will take greater risks in expressing themselves and revealing their knowledge in class. They will begin to feel competent in expanding their understanding of the interconnectedness of their worlds.

- ## Recognise that children live the oppressions of their families/communities

We all have oppressions and we all seek liberation from these oppressions. We carry around the hurts, put-downs and dashed hopes of our upbringing. We are often consumed with shame at not being able to resolve the emotional scars left by these experiences. Look for opportunities to broach the subject of personal loss with children. Current events are full of such opportunities given the war-torn world in which we live. By focusing on an individual case, consider the personal struggle of someone far away, and invite children to empathise and express their feelings. Teachers can liberate children by encouraging empathy and inviting them to read their own emotions.

- ## Allow children to identify their generative words and themes

Ask children to keep a personal log of words and issues that mean a lot to them. Encourage them to incorporate these words in their writings. Take a word and ask them to construct other words that have similar meanings or opposite meanings. Build classroom discussion around generative words that children produce. Work tirelessly at encouraging children to talk about what is relevant to them.

- **Honour children's products and celebrate their work**

Cultural ways of knowing are very deeply embedded in children's consciousness. Encourage them to explain what is meant by their words, activities or artefacts in their home and culture. Help them display their words, creations, drawings and artefacts in the classroom, and encourage them to incorporate them in their writings. Incorporate the culture of the children in lesson themes. Make explicit children's creation of knowledge and understanding.

- **Create a classroom that is multiliterate**

Encourage multiple understandings of words, and encourage multiple expressions of beliefs, perspectives and understanding. Say, 'Can anyone tell us another word for or another way of looking at this?' Remember that children seek to be powerful in the many realities of the postmodern world. Encourage multiple competencies and see all forms of expression and interaction as requiring the ability to read the world of the new childhood.

References

Ashton-Warner, S. (1971) *Teacher*. New York: Bantam Books.

Delpit, L. (1995) *Other people's children: Cultural conflict in the classroom*. New York: The New Press.

Dixon-Krauss, L. (1996) 'Classroom instruction', in L. Dixon-Krauss (ed.) *Vygotsky in the classroom: Mediated literacy instruction and assessment*. White Plains, NY: Longman.

Finn, P.J. (1999) *Literacy with an attitude: Educating working-class children in their own self-interest*. Albany, NY: State University of New York Press.

Freire, P. (1994) *Education for critical consciousness*. New York: The Continuum Publishing Company. (Original work published 1969.)

Freire, P. (1997) *Pedagogy of the oppressed* (Twentieth anniversary edition) (M.B. Ramos trans.). New York: Continuum Press. (Original work published 1968.)

Kincheloe, J.K. (2002) 'The complex politics of McDonald's and the new childhood: Colonizing kidworld', in G.S. Cannella & J.L. Kincheloe (eds) *Kidworld: Childhood studies, global perspectives and education*. New York: Peter Lang.

Loveless, T. (2002) *The 2002 Brown Center Report on American Education: How well are American students learning?* Washington, DC: The Brookings Institution.

Morris, W. (ed.) (1977) *The America Heritage Dictionary of the English Language*. Atlanta: Houghton Mifflin Company.

Ogbu, J.U. (1991) 'Low school performance as an adaptation: The case of blacks in Stockton, California', in M.A. Gibson & J.U. Ogbu (eds) *Minority status and schooling: A comparative study of immigrant and involuntary minorities*. New York: Garland Publishing Inc.

Steinberg, S.R. & Kincheloe, J.L. (1998) 'No more secrets: Kinderculture, information saturation, and the postmodern child', in S.R. Steinberg & J.L. Kincheloe (eds) *Kinderculture: The corporate construction of childhood* Boulder, CO: Westview Press.

Vygotsky, L.M. (1962) *Thought and language* (E. Hanfmann & G. Vaker trans.). Cambridge, MA: The MIT Press. (Original work published 1934.)

Willis, P. (1977) *Learning to labor: How working class kids get working class jobs*. New York: Columbia University Press.

Index

Italic page numbers indicate figures and illustrations not included in the text page range.